THE IPHONE 11 US

C000172092

Your Complete iPhone 11 Manual for Beginners, New iPhone 11 Users and Seniors

Tech Analyst

Copyright @2020

TABLE OF CONTENT

Introduction

The iPhone 11, one of the latest additions to the Apple iPhone family, is something most of us have been looking forward to since the announcement during the keynote presentation of the Apple company in the Worldwide Developer Conference held on June 13, 2019. The iPhone was launched alongside the iPhone 11 Pro and iPhone 11 Pro Max. The company started shipping the phones to customers on September 20, 2019. These new releases are updates to the iPhone XR, XS and XS Max devices that have been phased out of production by the Apple company, although still in sales. In this same period, we witnessed the launch of iOS 13, which came with several features enough to get users excited. While other devices before the iPhone 11 will need to download and install the iOS 13 software to their phones, you will not need to worry about the download as the new phones come pre-installed with the latest software. In this book, we have covered everything you need to know about the features and functions of the iOS 13 and iPhone 11 along with the latest tips and tricks to operate your device like a pro.

Additions to iOS 13

Siri

Siri has also been upgraded to be able to read out incoming messages on your device using the Airpods, and you can also give a response to the received message instantly using Siri. You do not need to use the wake word for this function to work, and another fantastic thing is that third-party messaging apps that have the Sirikit inbuilt will also have this feature. There is also the **Share Audio Experience** that you can use to share music faster with others through the Airpods. Siri can now play from over 100,000 radio stations all over the world using the Live radio feature that comes with a sleep timer. Finally, create your routines using the Suggested Automations located in the Siri shortcuts

Messages

The Messages app witnessed a significant improvement in this upgrade. You now have the feature to automatically share your profile picture and name with people when you begin to converse with them. Searching inside the Message app has also been made easier. Just click on the search bar in your message app, and it will show you recent messages, photos, people and other options. The search results tend to be more refined as you type to narrow down to the item you need.

Dark Mode

Once you update your device to the iOS 13, you will begin to enjoy the new dark mode features. The dark mode gives your phone a dark background and highlights on the phone's iOS and all the default Apple apps like messages, emails, and other apps. Apple has also asked developers to include this feature in third-party apps, and so, very soon, you will be able to enjoy this feature on other non-Apple apps. You have the option of either setting this mode permanently or modifying it to suit a particular time and period. You will see do this later in this book.

Swipe Typing

This is another feature introduced alongside the dark mode feature. I will go into full detail in a later part of this book.

Photos and Cameras

The camera app now has a new feature known as **High Key Mono,** a lighting effect with the portrait camera mode. You can also decide how intense you want the light to be by using the editing features to make your skin look smooth and bright to the eyes similar to what you see done with the moving lights found in a studio. The image editing feature of the photo's app has a swipe-based control as well as a new design. Now, you can use the same settings you use for stills to also edit your videos. Not only that, you can now rotate videos and also add filters. The Photo library has also been equipped to discover and delete duplicate copies of a single photo while it selects the ones that Apple will regard as your best shots. The images are then organized by months, day, or year, and you can see them in a new album view.

Another addition is that the live videos and photos are now on autoplay in the new photos tab, and you can now see the event, location or holiday, etc. for that photo within this same tab. On the photo tab, you will also see the new birthday mode that allows you to view pictures of celebrants on their birthdays. Now, you will see all your screen recordings in a single place, which makes it more organized and saves time used in searching all over the app.

Accessibility

Permit me to say that the addition of voice control is the most significant accessibility change that we see in the iOS 13, and this feature makes it easy for you to control your smartphone using your voice. The Siri speech recognition algorithm is used to confirm that the sound belongs to the authorized user before allowing access to the phone. You can also include custom words of your choice. No need to worry about personal data as the system leverages on device processing to keep your details safe.

Improvement to FaceTime

The iOS 13 also brought some improvements to the FaceTime video calls, especially in positioning the eye while on calls. The FaceTime software makes use of ARKit first to scan your face and then softly modify your eyes' position in a way that it will seem as if you are making direct eye contact with your caller rather than just starring at your screen.

Privacy

Apple has always been known to be particular about the privacy of its users, and we did not expect any less for iOS 13. Following the new granular controls, you can now decide apps that should have access to your location data. When you launch an app for the first time, you will see the option to either allow the app to access your location only once or for all the times that you may need to use the app. Apps will no longer be able to access your location through Bluetooth and Wi-fi without your permission. You are now able to choose persons that can see the location details of your photos. Each time you attempt to share your photos through the photo app, you will select whether the receiver should be given access to view the location the photo was shot in or not.

Performance

You will experience better performance on the new iOS 13 than was available with previous versions. Apple's Craig Federighi stated during the presentation that there would be a 30 percent increase in speed when using the FaceID to unlock your device. Apps updates have also been cut down by 60% while the size of apps downloads will be smaller by 50%. You will also experience a faster speed when launching apps than before.

Warnings for Active Subscription

On an attempt to delete an app you downloaded via in-app purchase from the Apple store, you will get a notification alerting you of the active subscription. You can then choose if you want to continue with your action or not.

Find My

In this new software upgrade, we saw that the **Find My Friend** and **Find My iPhone** features were collapsed into a single app called the **Find My** app. With this app, you can even find Lost devices regardless of whether they are offline by making use of the phone's Bluetooth connection.

Animoji and Memoji

Several new features are now available for Animojis and Memojis like glasses, makeup, hats, jewelry, and being able to change the look of your teeth. Your character can even wear Airpods. On your device keyboard, you can quickly access default Memoji stickers that you can share on apps like WeChat, Messages, and Mails.

Health App

Every function available on the new Watch OS health app is also in the iPhone 11 and all iOS 13 devices, functions like menstrual cycle tracking and the activity trends. On the main app, you will see a summary view where your notifications will be displayed as well as a highlight section to show your health and fitness data over time. Through machine learning, the app can show you things that are very important to your personal life.

Sign in with Apple

You will enjoy using this feature as it is an easy and fast way for you to sign in to services and apps without the need to reveal your social media login details. This feature authenticates your sign-ins using your Apple ID while ensuring that you do not disclose your details. This new service uses the TouchID and FaceID as well as a 2-factor authentication system. If you need to verify your login attempt into any app, Apple will create a random email address linked to your primary email address where the verification mail is sent and then redirected to your primary email address.

Apple Maps

Before now, the Apple map had limited functions for its users, unlike the Google map. However, there have been several alterations and additions like adding beaches, roads, buildings along with heightened details. There is also a new Favorite feature on your main screen, as well as organizing all your favorites and planned trips into a collection menu. We now have what Apple called the **Look Around,** just like Google's **Streetview,** so that you can see what a location looks like before you physically visit. You will learn use this feature in a later part of this guide. Another thing is that you can now share your ETA with your family and friends, receive updated flight information, real-time updates on the availability of public transportations, and the improved Siri navigation.

CarPlay

On your CarPlay app, you will notice the main screen called the **Dashboard,** where you will find controls for podcasts or music playback. You will also see basic maps information as well as control your HomeKit devices like garage door opener from this app. Apple Music is also modified to make it easy to find music. There is also a new calendar app to show a quick view of the day when embarking on a journey.

Reminders

You can now add in times, dates, and attachments into the reminders app. The app has also been integrated with the Messages app to allow both apps to communicate together. What this means is that whenever you set a reminder about a contact, this reminder will pop up the next time you message this contact. Siri has also been integrated into the reminders app. When typing words, Siri will give some related suggestions to what you are typing. Siri has also been configured to read out your reminders, and so, when chatting in the messaging app, Siri notifies you of things it assumes you should remember.

CHAPTER 1

Chapter 1: Getting Started:

Set Up Your iPhone 11

Setting up your device is the first and most crucial step to getting started with your iPhone 11. Follow these steps for a seamless experience.

1. Firstly, you need to power on your device. To do this, press and hold the side button. Now, you will see **"Hello"** in various languages.

   Note: From the Hello screen, you can activate the **VoiceOver or Zoom Option,** which is helpful for the blind or those with low vision.

2. Swipe up on your screen to begin set up.

3. A prompt will come up to select your language and country/region. You must choose the correct details as this will affect how information like date and time etc. appears on your device.

4. Next is to manually set up your iPhone by tapping **"Set up Manually."** You can choose the **"Quick Start"** option if you own another iOS 11 or later device and then follow the onscreen instruction. Proceed with the manual setup if you do not have any other iOS devices.

5. Now, you have to connect your phone to a cellular or Wi-Fi network to activate your device and continue with the setup. You should have inserted the SIM card before turning on the phone if going with the cellular network option. To connect to a Wi-Fi network, simply tap the name of your Wi-fi network. If there is a security lock on the Wi-fi, the screen will prompt you for the password before it connects.

6. At this stage, you can turn on the Location services option to give access to apps like **Maps** and **Find My**. You can always turn off this option whenever you want. I have included a guide on how to enable or disable location services in a later part of this book.

7. Next is to set up your Face ID. The face ID feature allows you to authorize purchases and unlock your devices using the registered face. To set up a face ID, tap **"Continue"** and follow the instructions on the screen. You can push this to a later time by selecting "**Set Up Later in Settings**."

8. Whether you set up Face ID now or later, you will be required to create a four-digit passcode to safeguard your data. This passcode is needed to access Touch ID and Apple Pay. Tap **"Passcode Option"** if you will rather set up a four-digit passcode, custom passcode, or even no passcode.

9. If you have an existing iTunes or iCloud backup, or even an Android device, you can restore the backed-up data to your new phone or move data from the old phone to the new iPhone. Choose the appropriate option on the **Apps and Data** screen to move data from your old device to the new one. In the absence of any backup or if this is your first device, select **"Don't Transfer Apps & Data."**

10. To continue, you will need to enter your Apple ID. If you have an existing Apple account, enter the ID and password to sign in. In case you don't have a current Apple ID or may have forgotten the login details, select **"Don't have an Apple ID or forget it."** If you belong to the class that has multiple Apple IDs, you should click on **"Use different Apple IDs for iCloud & iTunes."**

11. To proceed, you need to accept iOS terms and conditions.

12. Next is to set up Siri and other services needed on your device. Siri needs to learn your voice, so you will need to speak a few words to Siri at this point. You can also set up the iCloud keychain and Apple Pay at this point.

13. Set up screen time. Screen time will let you know the amount of time you spend on your device. You can also set time limits for your daily app usage. You will find a detailed guide on setting up screen time in a later part of this book

14. Now turn on automatic update and other essential features.

15. Click on **"Get Started"** to complete the process. And now, you can explore and enjoy your device.

Transfer Content to your iPhone from an Android Phone

You can move contents to your device from an Android mobile phone only when you first activate the device or after a factory reset. To do this, follow the steps above until you get to the **Apps and Data** screen.

- Then connect the Android device to an active wi-fi.

- Download and install the **"Move to iOS"** app on the android.

- Open the app on your android device.

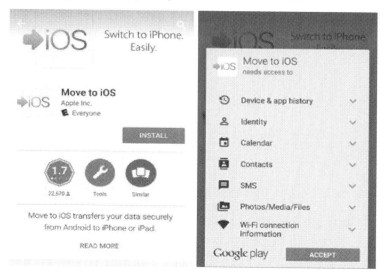

- Go to the iPhone SE, under **Apps and Data,** click on **"Move Data from Android."**

- Click on **Continue** on the two phones.

- Then follow the instructions you see on the screen to move data from the Android to the iPhone.

Buttons and Sockets on iPhone 11

Side Button: This is the first button by the top right side of the phone.

Use this button to power on the device and turn on the screen lock.

Silent Mode Key: This is the sliding key at the top left side of your phone. Move this key up or down to switch on or off the silent mode. The silent mode will deactivate sound notification on your phone.

Volume Keys: Use the key to increase or reduce volumes for calls, music, or the ring volume. You can also use it to mute an incoming call alert.

Camera lens: This function is for taking pictures or videos.

Lightning port: this is the socket at the bottom of the device used to charge the device or to plug in a headset for a handsfree call or listen to music.

Charge the Battery for the iPhone 11

- Connect the phone charger to a power socket and then connect the USB side to the lightning port at the bottom of the phone.
- To know that your battery is charging, you will see the battery charging icon displayed at the top of the screen.
- At the top right side of the screen, you will see your battery level. The more the colored section, the more power the device has and vice versa.

Turn on iPhone 11

The following steps will show you turn on the iPhone 11:

- Press the **Side** button until the iPhone comes on.
- Once you see the Apple logo, release the button and allow your iPhone to reboot for about 30 seconds.
- Once the iPhone is up, you will be required to input your password if you have one.

Turn off iPhone 11

Follow the steps below to turn off your iPhone 11:

- Hold both the volume down and the side button at the same time.
- Release the buttons once you see the power off slider.
- Move the slider to the right for the phone to go off.
- You may also use the side and volume up button. However, you may take a screenshot in error rather than shut down the phone.

Going Home on your iPhone 11

- Regardless of where you are on your iPhone 11, swipe your phone screen from the bottom up to return to the home screen.

Choose Ringtone on the iPhone 11

- From the Home screen, go to **Settings.**
- Click on **Sounds & Haptics.**

- Then click on **Ringtone.**
- You may click on each of the ringtones until you find the one that you want.
- Select the one you like then click on the "**< Back"** key at the top left of the screen.
- Slide the page from the bottom up to return to the Home screen.

Choose Message Tone
- From the Home screen, go to **Settings.**
- Click on **Sounds & Haptics.**
- Then click on "**Text Tone."**
- You may click on each of the message tones until you find the one that you want.
- Select the one you like then click the "**< Back"** key at the top left of the screen.

Set/ Change Language
- From the Home screen, click on the **Settings** option.
- Click on **General.**
- Then click on **Language and Region.**
- Click on **iPhone Language** to give you options of available languages.
- Choose your language from the drop-down list and tap **Done.**
- A pop-up will appear on your screen, prompting you to confirm your action. Click on **Change to (Selected) Language.**

Set/ Change Date/ Time

- From the Home screen, click on the **Settings** option.
- Click on **General**.
- Then click on **Date & Time.**
- On the next screen, beside the **"Set Automatically"** option, move the switch right to turn it on.

Chapter 2: Apple ID on iPhone 11

Your Apple ID is the account that you use to access iOS services like Apple Music, FaceTime, iCloud, iMessage, and more. You can use a single Apple ID and password to sign in to all your Apple services.

- Open the **Settings** app.
- At the top of your screen, click on **Sign in to your iPhone.**

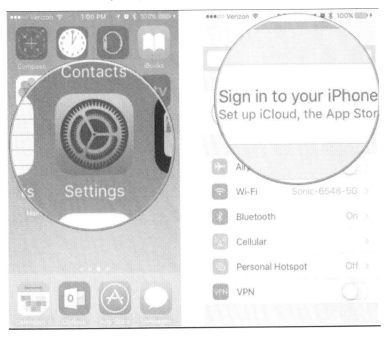

- Choose **Don't have an Apple ID or forgot it?**
- A pop-up will appear on the screen, click on **Create Apple ID.**
- Input your date of birth and click on **Next.**
- Then input your first name and last name, then click on **Next.**
- The next screen will present you with the email address option. Click on **"Use Your Current Email Address"** if you want to use

an existing email or click on **"Get a Free iCloud Email Address"** if you want to create a new email.

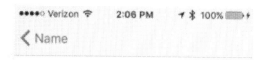

Email Address

Use your current email address >

Get a free iCloud email address >

- If using an existing email address, input your email address and password.
- If creating a new one, select the option and type your preferred email and password.
- Verify the new password.
- The next option is to select 3 Security Questions from the list and provide answers.
- You have to agree to the device's Terms and conditions to proceed.
- Select either **Merge** or **Don't Merge** to sync the data saved on iCloud from reminders, Safari, calendars, and contacts.
- Click **OK** to confirm that **"Find My is turned on."**

Chapter 3: iCloud

iCloud is a cloud computing and storage service from Apple. You can save your photos, contacts, videos, documents, backups, etc. on the iCloud and access it at anytime using your Apple ID. All Apple users get free 5GB storage. You will need to purchase more storage space once you exhaust the free space.

Sign in to iCloud

- Go to the **Settings app.**
- At the top of your screen, click on **Sign in to your iPhone**.

- Enter your Apple ID email address and password.
- Then click on **Sign In.**
- The next screen will ask for your device passcode if you set up one.
- Set the iCloud Photos the way up like them.
- Switch **Apps using iCloud** on or off, however you want it.

Sign Out of iCloud on Your iPhone

- From the **Settings app,** click on **your name.**
- Click on **Sign Out** at the bottom of the screen.

- Input your Apple ID password then select **Turn Off.**
- Chose the data you will like to keep a copy of on your iPhone and move the switch on.
- At the top right corner of your screen, click on **Sign Out.**
- Click on **Sign Out** again to confirm your decision.

Use iCloud Backup

To use the iCloud backup, ensure that your device is connected to Wi-fi before you begin. You also need to connect your phone to a charging point while the process is on. To back up, follow the steps below

- Go to **Settings,** click on your name, then tap **iCloud.**
- Toggle on **iCloud Backup.**
- Then click on **Back Up Now.**
- On this same screen, you will find the date and time of the last backup.

Share a Calendar on iPhone via iCloud

To share your calendar on your iPhone, it is essential to first of all turn on the iCloud for calendar option. Kindly follow the steps below:

- On your iPhone, go to **Settings.**
- Click on your device name at the top of the screen, and select **iCloud.**
- Then turn on **Calendars.**

After you must have done this, you can now share your calendar by following these steps:

- Open the **Calendar** app on your device.
- At the bottom of your screen, select **Calendars.**
- You will see an (i) icon next to the calendar you want to share, click on the icon.
- Select the **Add Person** option on the screen, then pick the people you wish to share the calendar with.
- Tap **Add,** followed by **Done** at the top of your screen.

Synchronize using iCloud

To synchronize your phone details on iCloud, follow the steps below:

- Click on your Apple ID in the **Settings** app.

- Click on **iCloud**.

- Scroll down to **iCloud Drive** and move the switch left or right to enable or disable.

- Under **iCloud**, click on **Photos.**

- Scroll down to **Upload to My Photo Stream** and slide left to right to activate or disable.

Troubleshoot if iCloud isn't Working

If your iCloud isn't working, follow the steps below to troubleshoot:

- Ensure the Wi-fi is connected and reliable as this is usually the main reason for iCloud backup not responding.

- Once done, confirm that you have sufficient space in the cloud. Apple gives you only 5G free. If you have used up the free space, clear the files you don't need or back them up with iTunes, then remove them from the iCloud backup.

- If you do not wish to delete any information, the next step will be to purchase an additional room in the iCloud. The pricing is shown below: 50 GB per month: 0.99 USD

  200GB per month: 2.99 USD

  2 TB per month: 9.99 USD

- Finally, remove any irrelevant data from the iPhone before you perform the iCloud backup.

Chapter 4: Use Siri on iPhone 11

Apples' virtual assistant is a delight to work with, everyone loves Siri, and most of the time you spend with her involves getting an answer, but she can do more than answer questions.

Set up Siri on iPhone 11

To use Siri on your iPhone, you have to set it up like you set up the Face ID. Find below the steps to do this on your iPhone.

- Click on **Siri & Search** from the **Settings** app.
- Toggle on the switch beside **"Press Side Button for Siri."**
- A pop-up notification will appear on the screen, select **"Enable Siri."**
- Toggle on the switch beside **"Listen to Hey Siri"** option and follow the instructions you see on the screen of your iPhone.

 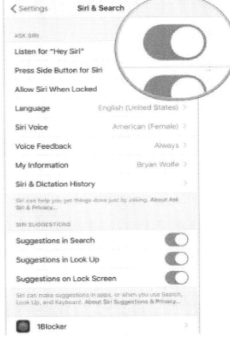

- To use Siri when your phone is locked, activate the **"Allow Siri When Locked"** option.

- Click on **Language** and select the desired language.

- Click on the **< Siri & Search** button at the top left of the screen to go back.

- Click on **Siri Voice.**

- Select **Accent and Gender.**

- Click on the **< Siri & Search** button at the top left of the screen.

- Click on **Voice Feedback** and choose your preferred option.

- Click on **< Siri & Search** at the top left of the screen.

- Select **My Information.**

- Click on the contact of choice. Save your contact details if you want to set yourself as the owner of the phone. The phone will use your data for various voice control functions like navigating home screen. You can create yourself on the contact by following the steps given in creating contacts.

- Choose the desired application.

- Navigate to **"Search and Siri Suggestions"** and move the slider to the left/ right to turn on or off.

- Now Siri is set up and ready to be used.

Activate Siri on the iPhone 11

There are two ways to activate Siri on your iPhone.

- **Voice option.** If you enabled "Hey Siri," then you can begin by saying "Hey Siri" and then ask Siri any question.

- The second option is to use the side button. To wake Siri, press the side button, and ask your questions. Once you release the side button, Siri stops listening.

Exit Siri

To exit Siri, follow the simple step below.

- Press the side button or swipe up from the bottom of the display to exit Siri.

Add Siri Shortcuts

Siri now has an app which makes it easier and faster to assign functions to the virtual assistant.

- Click on the **Shortcut app** to launch it.
- After which you click on **Create Shortcuts** to create a simple type of shortcut.
- Then click on **Create Shortcuts** to create a simple type of shortcut.
- With the **automation** tab, your device can intelligently react to context as they change. For instance, you can customize the shortcut to play a particular song each time you get home or design the button to automatically send your location to your partner once you leave the office at the end of the day.
- In the **Gallery** tab, you will find a range of predefined shortcuts to give you some inspiration in designing yours, or you can even make use of the predefined shortcuts.

Play Live Radio Through Siri

Siri has access to over 100,000 radio stations from different parts of the world. You can ask Siri to play live radio stations by saying, "Hey Siri, "play [name of radio station] radio station." So long as Siri can access the requested radio station, you will hear the station play instantly.

Chapter 5: Use Screen Time

This feature helps you to monitor how much time you spend on your device. On the screen time option, you will see the complete details on the hours spent on your iPhone.

Enable Screen Time

- Open the **Settings** app.
- Click on **Screen time.**
- Click on **Turn on Screen Time** to enable the feature.

Set App Limits

Use the **App Limit** feature of the Screen Time to set the length of time you want to spend on certain apps. Follow the steps below to guide you.

- Go to the Settings app on your device
- Then click on **Screen Time**

- Navigate and click on **App Limits.**

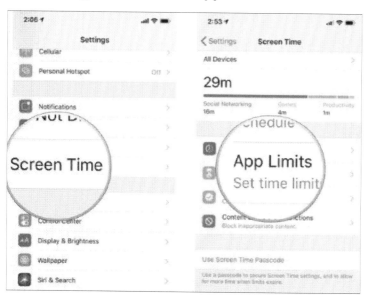

- Then select **Add Limit.**

In iOS 13, you can now group similar apps with the same app limit. What this means is that you can bring Spotify, Twitter, and Fortnite together to have a combined total of 6 hours every day. As soon as the limit is exhausted, a splash will appear on your screen notifying you that the set limit is exhausted. You will also get the option to ignore the deadline for the remainder of the day or 15 minutes only.

Chapter 6: The Control Centre

Control center gives you instant access to things you use most on your phone like taking pictures, controlling your Apple TV and lots more.

Access Control Center

- From the right side of the notch, swipe down to view the control center.
- Click on a function to either open it or enable/disable.
- Move your finger up the function to modify its settings.

Modify Access to Control Center From Within Apps

You may choose to access the control center when using other apps.

Here is how to enable or disable this option:

- Go to **Settings**, click on **Control Center.**
- Beside the **"Access Within Apps"** option, move the switch to the right or left to turn it on or off.

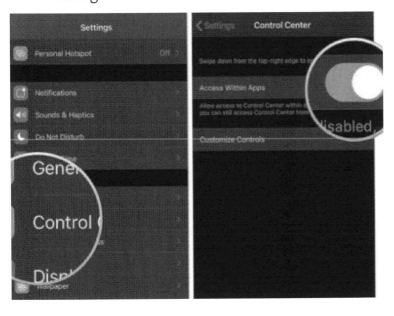

Customize Control Center

- Go to **Settings,** click on **Control Center.**

- Click on **Customize Controls.**

- Click on ⊖ sign beside the functions you want to remove, then tap **Remove** to delete.

- To add icon under **More Controls,** click on the ⊕ sign at the left side of the icons.

- Click on the ▤ icon beside each function and drag the function to the position that you want.

- And you are done.

Access Paired Bluetooth Devices from Control Center

You can easily access paired devices on your iPhone without having to exit a particular app. If you need to pair a device to Bluetooth, follow the steps below from anywhere on your phone:

- Go to the control center, make a swipe gesture from the right top side of the iPhone down to go to the control center.

- You can 3D Touch or click and hold down on the wireless connections block at the top right side of the screen to expand it.

- 3D Touch or Tap and hold the Bluetooth button at the right of the screen.

- On the next screen, you have all the Bluetooth devices, those previously paired, and those available.

- Choose the one you want to connect with.

Connect to Wi-Fi Through the Control Center

Here is a faster and direct way to connect to wi-fi that does not require launching the settings app. You also do not need to leave a current app.

- Go to the control center, make a swipe gesture from the right top side of the iPhone down to go to the control center.

- You can 3D Touch, or click and hold down on the wireless connections block at the top right side of the screen to expand it.

- 3D Touch or Tap and hold the Wi-Fi button on the left side of your screen.

- The next screen will display all nearby Wi-fi networks that have been paired previously regardless of their connection status.
- Choose your preferred one to connect.

Chapter 7: Apple Pay

Apple Pay allows you to make secure and contactless purchases on the web, in-store and on your iPhone. The service also allows you to receive and send money to your family and friends right from the Message app.

Set Up Apple Pay

- You need to add your card, either debit, credit, or prepaid cards to the Wallet app on your iPhone.
- Ensure that you are signed in to iCloud using your Apple ID.
- Using Apple Pay on more than one device will require you to add your card to each of the devices.

Follow the steps below to add your card to Apple Pay:

- Open the Wallet app and click on ⊕
- Follow the instructions on the screen to add a new card. On iPhone 11, you can add as much as 12 cards. You may be asked to add cards linked to your iTunes, cards you have active on other devices, as well as cards that you removed recently. Choose the cards that fall into the requested categories and enter the security code for each card.
- Tap **Next** and the information you inputted will go through your bank or card issuer for verification and confirmation.
- Once the card is verified successfully, click **Next** to begin using Apple Pay.

Check out with Apple Pay

After shopping and you need to make your payments at a checkout terminal, the steps below would guide you on check out using Apple Pay:

- Double-press the side button to open the **Apple Pay** screen.
- Look at the iPhone screen to verify the attempt with Face ID (or enter your passcode).
- Then place the iPhone near the payment terminal.
- If you're using Apple Pay Cash, double-press the side button to approve the payment.

Chapter 8: Basic Functions

Wake and Sleep Your iPhone 11

Waking and sleeping your iPhone 11 will preserve your battery life and make it long-lasting; here are the steps to wake and put your iPhone 11 to sleep.

- There are two ways to wake your iPhone 11 and to see the lock screen; either tap the screen or just picking up the device and glancing at it can wake the iPhone 11.

- From the lock screen, you can use either the camera or the flashlight by a simple gesture. Tap and hold the individual icon until you hear a click sound.

- Press the side button to make the iPhone 11 go to sleep. With the Apple Leather Folio case designed for the iPhone 11, open the case to wake and close the case to sleep your device.

Turn PIN On or Off

- From **Settings,** click on **Phone.**
- At the bottom of the screen, click on the **SIM PIN.**
- Turn the icon beside SIM PIN to the left or right to put off or on.
- Put in your PIN and click on **Done**. The default PIN for all iPhone 11 is 0000.

Change Device PIN

- From **Settings,** click on **Phone.**
- At the bottom of the screen, click on the **SIM PIN.**
- To change the PIN, click on **Change PIN**.
- Type in your current PIN and click **Done.**

- On the next screen, type in the new 4-digit PIN and tap **Done.**
- The next screen will require you to input the PIN again and click on **Done.**

Unblock Your PIN

If you enter a wrong PIN 3 consecutive times, it will block the PIN temporarily. Follow the steps to unblock:

- On the home screen, click on **Unlock.**
- Put in the PUK and click on **OK.**
- Set a new 4-digit PIN and click **OK.**
- Input the PIN again and confirm.

Customize Raise to Wake

- From **Settings,** go to **Display & Brightness.**
- On the next screen, besides **Raise to Wake,** move the slider left or right to enable or disable.

Arrange Home Screen Icons

Follow the steps below to arrange the icons on your home screen:

- Press and hold any icon until all the icons begin to wiggle.
- Drag the icons into your desired position.
- Tap either the **Done** button at the upper right side of the screen or swipe up to exit the wiggle mode.

Check Battery Percentage

The iPhone does not give room to see your phone's battery percentage, but you can still get a peek to see your battery percentage. To do this,swipe up to display the control center. Once the control center is open, you will see the battery percentage at the top right corner.

Control Bluetooth

- From **Settings,** go to **Bluetooth.**

- Move the switch beside **Bluetooth** to switch on or switch off Bluetooth.

- To pair with a mobile device, put on the Bluetooth, then click on the device you want to pair and follow the steps on the screen to link.

Confirm Software Version

- From **Settings,** go to **General** and click on **About.**

- You will see your device version besides **Version** on the next screen.

Update Software

- From **Settings,** go to **General** and click on **Software Update.**

- If there is a new update, it will show on the next screen.

- Then follow the screen instruction to update the software.

Control Flight Mode

- From the top right side of the screen, slide downwards.

- Tap the airplane icon to enable or disable flight mode.

Choose Night Shift Settings
- From the **Settings** app, click on **Display & Brightness.**
- Click on **Night Shift** at the bottom of your screen.

- Toggle on the switch beside **Scheduled,** then follow the instruction on the screen to select a duration for the Night Shift.

- To enable Night Shift immediately, toggle on the button beside **Manually Enable Until Tomorrow.**

- Below the **Color Temperature** option, pull the slider to the left or right until you get your desired color temperature.

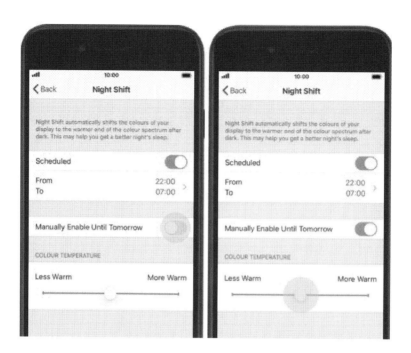

53

Chapter 9: Dark Mode

At times, the brightness of our phones can be blinding, especially when you pick up your phone in the early hours of the morning due to the bright white theme of your phone. There is now a new **dark mode** feature to help moderate the brightness of your phone. When this feature is active, all your system apps like the iMessage and Safari will be affected. Apple has also called on third-party app developers to design their apps with themes that are compatible with the dark mode.

Enable Dark Mode
The steps below will show you enable the Dark Mode.

- Go to the Settings app
- Click on **Display and Brightness**

- In the next screen, you will see options for **Light** and **Dark** under Appearance.
- Tap on any of the options you want to activate

Automatically Activate Dark Mode

You do not always need to go to the settings each time you need to activate the dark mode theme. You can set up your phone to automatically change to the bright theme in the day and the dark theme at night with the simple steps below:

- From the settings app, click on **Display and Brightness.**
- Scroll and toggle on the switch next to **Automatic.**
- By default, the menu will change to **Sunset to Sunrise.**
- If you want to change this selection, click on **Options** under the **Automatic** menu.
- **Sunset to Sunrise** uses your GPS location to activate the Dark mode feature once the sun goes down.
- You can select *Custom Schedule* and input your own desired time for the Dark Mode to kick in.

Set Your Wallpaper to React to Dark Mode

Wallpapers on your iPhone can react when your phone is on Dark Mode. The first step is to select a wallpaper that has a dynamic color-changing feature.

- From the settings app, click on **Wallpapers.**
- Select *Choose a New Wallpaper* and then click on *Stills*.
- Every wallpaper that reacts to Dark Mode has a bisected small circle mark at the right of your screen under each wallpaper.
- Each image has two sides, with the second side giving a display of how the wallpaper will look in Dark mode.

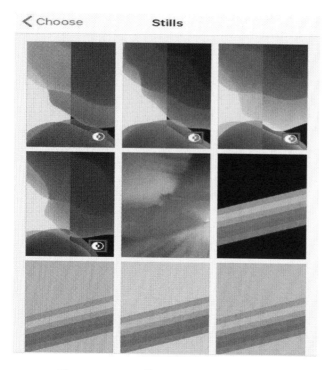

- To use a wallpaper outside these ones, go to the **Wallpaper menu.**

- Then click on *Dark Appearance Dims Wallpaper,* move the switch beside it to the right to enable this feature. Your wallpaper may not be as effective as the system wallpapers, but they will dim somewhat when the Dark mode is enabled.

Chapter 10: Notifications

Control Notification Options

- From Settings, go to **Notifications.**

- Click on **Show Preview** and set to **Always** to be able to preview notification on the lock screen.

- To set this to only when the device is not locked, click on the option **"When Unlocked."**

- To disable notification preview, select **"Never."**

- Click on the Back arrow at the top left of the screen.

Control Notification for Specific Apps

To choose notification settings for individual apps, follow below:

- From Settings, go to **Notifications.**

- Click on the specific application.

- On the next screen, beside **Allow Notifications,** move the slider left or right to enable or disable.

Customize Notification Grouping

- From Settings, go to **Notifications.**

- Click on the apps that you want to customize group notification.

- Scroll down the page and click on **Notification Grouping.**
- Choose your preference from the displayed option on your screen.

    ✓ **Automatic** if you want Siri to suggest how the notifications should be grouped.

    ✓ **By App** to group notifications by app.

    ✓ **Off** to disable notification grouping.

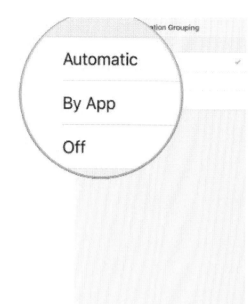

Chapter 11: Location Services

Enable Location Services/ GPS on your iPhone

- From the Home screen, choose the **Settings** option.

- Scroll towards the bottom of the page and click on **Privacy.**

- Then click on **Location Services** and toggle on the service.

- Toggle on all the apps that should have access to your location data.

- Once selected, chose the option **While Using the App.**

Turn Off Location Services on iPhone Selectively

If there are any apps, you will like to block from accessing your location, and you can quickly turn off location service for such apps by following the steps below.

- Open the settings app.

- Scroll towards the bottom of the page and click on **Privacy.**

- Then click on **Location Services** and toggle on the service.

- You will see all the apps that can and cannot access your location. For the apps you wish to access your location information, find such apps, click on them, and select **While**

Using the App. For apps that should not have access to your location details, click on the apps and choose **Never.** You can also use these steps for the system services that should not have access to your location information.

Turn Off Location Services on iPhone Completely

To stop sharing your location,

- Open the Settings app.
- Scroll towards the bottom of the page and click on **Privacy.**
- Then click on **Location Services** and toggle off the service.

Chapter 12: Camera

Use Camera

- From the Home screen, tap the Camera app.

- Move your finger left or right to take you to the **Photo** option, which is after **Video** by your left and before **Portrait** by your right.

- Click the flash icon ⚡ at the top of the screen to enable, if desired.

- Set the camera lens to point at the object you want to capture

- Draw two fingers apart/ together on the screen to zoom in or out

- Click on the shutter icon ⊚ to take a picture.

Use Video Recorder

- Open the camera app.

- Move your finger left or right to take you to the **Video** option, which is before **Photo** by your right.

- Set the camera lens to point at the object you want to capture.
- Click on the **Record** icon, which is the round icon at the bottom of the screen.
- Draw two fingers apart/ together on the screen to zoom in or out
- Tap the **Stop** icon at the bottom of the screen to stop the recording.

You can send a video clip or picture to another person as an MMS. To do this, follow the listed steps

- Open the **Photos** app.
- Go to the desired photo folder.
- Click on the desired video clip or picture.

- Tap the share button ⬆️ at the left bottom side of the screen.
- On the next screen, click on **Message.**
- On the **To** field, input the receiver's details.
- Click on the **Text** area to input your message.
- Once done, click on the Send button .

Send Video Clip or Picture in an Email

Follow the steps below to attach a video or picture with your email:
- Open the **Photos** app.
- Go to the desired photo folder.
- Click on the desired video clip or picture.
- Tap the share button ⬆️ at the left bottom side of the screen.
- On the next screen, click on **Mail.**
- On the **To** field, input the receiver's details.
- Input your email subject on the **Subject** field.
- Click on the **Text** area to input your email message.
- Once done, click on **Send** to deliver your email.

Use Lighting Mode Photo Effects

For pictures captured in portrait mode, your smartphone uses the dual camera to create a depth-of-the-field effect to give you a photo with a blurred background and sharp subject. Now, we have another new feature called the **High-Key Light Mono.** This is similar to the white and black effect of the Stage Light Mono, but this will only give you a white background as against a black and white background.

- Open the photo app and click on a portrait photo. Portrait photos have the **Portrait** label at the top left side of the image.
- Click on **Edit** at the top right corner to go into editing mode.

- Select the portrait icon in the tools at the bottom row then choose a lighting mode by sliding along the icons under the photos with your finger.

- After selecting a lighting mode like the High-Key Light Mono effect, a slider will show underneath the image.

- Move the slider up or down to modify the lighting effect intensity.

- Click on **Done** once you are satisfied with how the image looks.

Edit Voice Memos

If you have always wanted to be able to edit your voice memos, now you can with the steps below:

- Go to your recorded voice memo.

- Click on **Edit.**

- Pinch on your screen to zoom the waveform to give you better control and make it easy for you to scrub through recordings that are very long.

69

Edit Photos and Rotate Videos

Here is a simple guide to editing your photos:

- Launch the Photos app.

- Click on your desired photo and then click on **Edit**.

- The next screen will offer you several options to modify your photos. Swipe to explore your actions and adjust the sliders to view the changed look of your photos.

- This step also applies to your videos.

Apply Filter to a Video

The filter tool is similar to the one you use on Instagram.

- From the photo app, choose the video you wish to edit.

- Then click on **Edit at** the top right side of your screen.

- You will see the filter menu at the bottom of the screen.

- There are nine available filters that you can navigate through for a feel on how each will look on your video.

- Pick the filter you want, and a horizontal dial will appear under the selected filter.

- Slide the dial to adjust the level of intensity of that filter.
- Once you are satisfied with the outcome, click on **Done** at the bottom right side of your screen to effect the filter on your video.

Remove Location Details from your Photos

Each time you take photos on your smartphone, the GPS records the exact location the photo was shot. This helps you to view your photos based on location, especially when sorting out photoshoots. This also means that people who view your pictures on their photo app can see the place you took the photo. This poses security threats, especially when sharing images on social media or to a group that you have no personal relationship with. The good news is that you can remove the location details from your photos before sharing or select persons that should be able to view this information. Apart from photos, you can remove location details from your videos, movies and even multiple images sent via messages, Facebook, Mail, and so on with the steps below:

- After shooting your photos, go to the folder where the picture is stored.
- For a single video or photo, click on the video or photo to open then click on **Share** .
- For multiple videos and pictures, click on **Select,** then select all the items for sharing before you click on the **Share** button.
- On the next screen, click on **Options.**
- Move the switch beside **Location** to the left to disable this feature.

- Tap **Done.**
- Then pick the method you want to use in sending your pictures.

Note: each time you want to share a video or picture, remember to disable location, and the option is only available when sharing the photos or videos directly from your Photo app. Disabling the location feature when sharing does not remove location details from the images and videos saved on your phone.

Manually Add or Remove Music and Videos

To manually manage your music and videos, you will have to copy the video files and music tracks to the iPhone from the iTunes Library. Follow the steps below to do this:

- Connect your device to your computer or Mac.
- Launch the iTunes app.
- Manually move the media to the left side of the window.
- Release the media on top of the iPhone (Under **Devices**).
- Now drag any of the items from the main window to the sidebar to add to your iPhone from iTunes.

Chapter 13: Calls and Contacts

Answer Call

- Tap any of the volume keys to silence the call notification when a call comes in.
- If the screen lock is active, slide right to answer the call.
- Click on Accept, if there is no screen lock.
- Tap the end call button at the bottom of the screen once done.

Call a Number

- Tap the Phone icon on the left.
- Click on Keypads to show the keypads.
- Input the number you want to call then press the call icon.
- Tap the end call button at the bottom of the screen once done.

Control Call Waiting

- From **Settings,** click on **Phone** then click on **Call Waiting.**

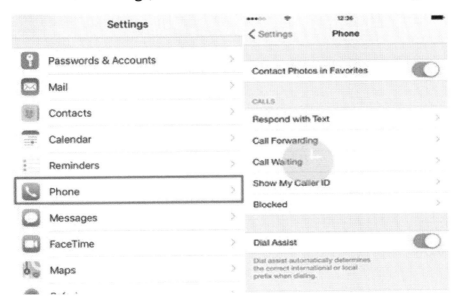

- Move the switch beside **Call Waiting** to the left or right to enable or disable.

Control Call Announcement

Your phone can be set to read out the caller's name when there is an incoming call. The number must be in your address book for this to work.

- From **Settings,** go to **Phone** then click on **Announce Call.**
- Select **Always** if you want this feature when silent mode is off.
- Choose **Headphones & Car** to activate when your device is connected to a car or a headset.
- The **Headphones Only** option will be for when the device is connected to a headset.
- Select **Never** if you do not wish to turn off this feature.

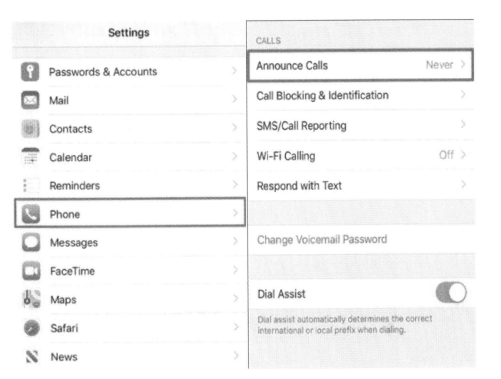

Add Contacts

- Open the **Contacts** app.

- Then click on ✛ > **Add** icon at the top right side of your screen.

- Enter the details of your contact, including the name, phone number, address, etc.

- Once done inputting the details, tap **Done** to save.

Merge Similar Contacts

- Open the **Contacts** app on your home screen.

- Click on the contact you want to merge and click on **Edit.**

- At the bottom of the screen, click on **Link Contact.**

- Choose the other contact you want to link.

- Click on **Link** at the top right side of the screen.

Copy Contact from Social Media and Email Accounts

- Open the Settings app and click on **Accounts and Password.**

- Click on the account, e.g., Gmail.

- Toggle on **Contacts.**

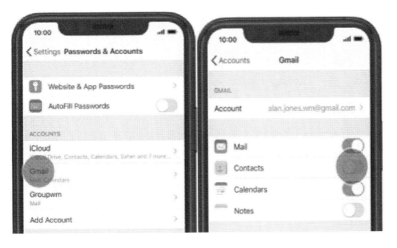

Save Your Voicemail Number

- Once you insert your SIM into your new device, it automatically saves your voicemail number.

Add a Caller to your Contact

- On your call log, click on a phone number.

- You will see options to **Message, Call, Create New Contact, or Add to Existing Contact**.

- Select **Create New Contact.**

- Enter the caller's name and other information you have.

- At the top right hand of the screen, click on **Done**.

Add a Contact After Dialing The Number on The Keypad

- Manually type in the numbers on the phone app using the number keys.

- Click on ⊕ on the left side of the number.

- Click on **Create New Contact.**

- Enter the caller's name and other information you have.

- Or click on **Add to Existing Contact**. Find the contact name you want to add the contact to and click on the name.
- At the top right hand of the screen, click on **Done**.

Import Contacts

The iPhone allows you to import or move your contacts from your phone to the SIM card or SD card for either safekeeping or backup. See the steps below:

- From the Home screen, click on **Settings.**
- Select **Contacts.**
- Click on **Import SIM Contacts.**
- Chose the account where the contacts should be stored.
- Allow the phone to import the contacts to your preferred account or device.

Delete contacts

Follow the steps below to delete contact

- From the Home screen, tap on **Phone** to access the phone app.
- Select **Contacts.**
- Click on the contact you want to remove.
- You will see some options, select **Edit.**
- Move down to the bottom of your screen and click on **Delete Contact.**
- You will see a popup next to confirm your action. Click on **Delete Contact** again.
- The deleted contact will disappear from the available Contacts.

Silence Unknown Callers

A new feature called the "silence unknown callers" was added to iOS 13. You can now block spam calls without having to block each one individually. With this method, the caller is not permanently barred as their calls are sent straight to voicemail, and should you discover that a blocked call is not spam, you can go to your voicemail to listen to the message and call back whoever you need to contact. The steps below will show you enable the new call blocker:

- From the settings app, click on **Phone.**
- Navigate to *Silence Unknown Callers* and move the switch to the right to enable it.

This feature will automatically send unknown callers to voicemails and will give you less to worry about robocalls and spam calls.

Use and Manage Call Forwarding on your iPhone

With the Call Forwarding Unconditional (CFU) feature in the iPhone, calls will go straight to a separate phone number without the main device ringing. This is most useful when you do not wish to turn off ringer or disregard a call but also do not want to be distracted by such calls. To enable this feature, follow the steps below:

- Go to **Settings** from the home screen.
- Click on **Phone** then click on **Call Forwarding.**
- Select the **Forward To** option.
- Input the second number where you want to receive the calls. It could be your voicemail.

Apart from CFU, Call Forwarding Conditional (CFC) allows you to forward incoming calls to a different number if the call goes unanswered on your number. To enable this feature, you need to have the shortcodes for call forwarding then set the options to your preference. For these shortcodes, reach out to your carrier.

Cancel Call Forwarding on your iPhone
To cancel,

- Go to **Settings** then click on **Phone.**
- Click on **Call Forwarding.**
- Move the slider to switch off the feature.

Manage Caller ID Settings and Call Logs on your iPhone
You can decide to hide your caller ID when calling specific numbers. Follow the steps below to activate this.

- Go to **Settings** on the Home screen.
- Click on **Phone** then click on **Show My Caller ID.**
- Click on the switch next to **Show My Caller ID** to enable or disable the option.

When you disable the feature, the called party will not see your caller ID. This is usually for security or privacy reasons.

Reset Call Logs

For every call you make on your device, there is a log saved on the phone app. To reset the call log data, follow the steps below:

- Go to **Phones,** then click on **Recent>All>Edit.**
- Click on the **minus (-) sign** to delete calls individually.
- To delete the whole call log once, tap **Clear** then chose the **Clear All Recent** option.

Set Do Not Disturb

Your device can be in silent mode for a defined period. Even though your phone is in silent mode, you can set to receive notification from particular callers.

- Under **Settings,** click on **Do Not Disturb.**
- Toggle the switch next to **"Do Not Disturb"** to the right to enable this function.
- Toggle the switch next to **"Scheduled"** to the right. Then, follow instructions on your screen to set the period for the DND.
- Under **Silence**, select **"Always"** if you want your device to be permanently on silent mode.
- Select **"While iPhone is locked"** if you want to limit this to only when the phone is locked.
- Scroll down and click on **"Allow Calls from."**

- Chose the setting that meets your need to set the contacts that can reach you while on DND.
- Click on the back arrow at the top left of the screen.
- Scroll down to **Repeated Calls** and switch the button on or off as needed.
- Click on **"Activate"** under **"Do Not Disturb While Driving."**
- On the next screen, choose your preferred option.
- Click on the back button to return to the previous screen.
- Scroll down and select **"Auto Reply-To".**
- On the next screen, select the contacts you wish to notify that **Do Not Disturb While Driving** is on.
- Go back to the previous screen.
- Scroll down and select **Auto Reply,** then follow the instructions on the screen to set your auto-response message.

Chapter 14: Messages App

Set up your Device for iMessaging

- From the Settings app, go to **Messages**.

- Enable **iMessages** by moving the slider to the right.

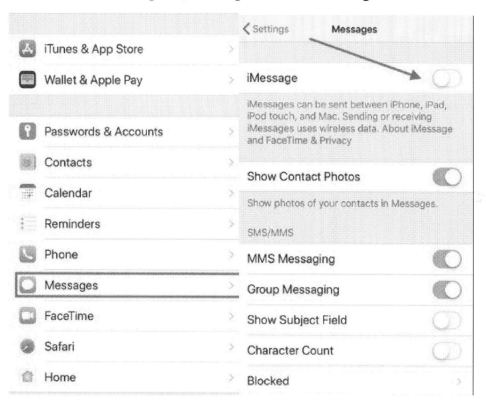

Set up Your Device for MMS

- From **Settings**, go to **Messages**.

- Enable **MMS Messaging** by moving the slider to the right.

Compose and Send iMessage

- From the Message icon, click on the new message option at the top right of the screen.

- Under the "**To**" field, type in the first few letters of the receiver's name.
- Select the receiver from the drop-down.
- You will see iMessage in the composition box only if the receiver can receive iMessage.
- Click on the **Text Input Field** and type in your message.
- Click on the send button beside the composed message.
- You will be able to send video clips, pictures, audios, and other effects in your iMessage.

Compose and Send SMS

- From the Message icon, click on the new message option at the top right of the screen.
- Under the "**To**" field, type in the first few letters of the receiver's name.
- Select the receiver from the drop-down.
- Click on the "**Text Input Field**" and type in your message.
- Click on the send button beside the composed message.

Compose and Send SMS with Pictures

- From the Message icon, click on the **New Message** option at the top right of the screen.
- Under the "**To**" field, type in the first few letters of the receiver's name.
- Select the receiver from the drop-down.
- Click on the **Text Input Field** and type in your message.

- Click the **Camera** icon on the left side of the composed message.
- From **Photos**, go to the right folder.
- Select the picture you want to send.
- Click **Choose** and then **Send.**

Create New Contacts from Messages On iPhone

- Go to the Messages app.
- Click on the conversation with the sender whose contact you want to add.
- Click on the sender's phone number at the top of the screen, then click on **Info**.
- On the next screen, click on the arrow by the top right side of your screen.
- Then click **Create New Contact**.
- Input their name and other details you have on them.
- At the top right hand of the screen, click on **Done**.

Hide Alerts in Message app on your iPhone

- Go to the **Message app** on your iPhone.

- Open the conversation you wish to hide the alert.

- Click on (i) at the upper right corner of the page.

- Among the options, one of them is '**Hide alerts**', move the switch to the right to turn on the option (the switch becomes green).

- Select **Done** at the right upper corner of your screen.

Set a Profile Picture and Name in iMessages

Setting a profile picture and name in iMessages saves users from first saving your contact details to decipher who sent a message. Follow the steps below to set this up.

- Open the messages app.

- Click on the ••• icon at the upper right corner of your screen.

- Then click on **Edit Name and Photo.**

- Select a profile picture and type in your last and first names.

- You can either create your own Memoji to use as your profile picture or select from available Animoji.

Specify View for your Profile Picture and Name in iMessages

You can choose who you will like to be able to view your profile picture and name. This setting is used to limit users who can access your details.

- Open the messages app.

- Click on the ⚫ icon at the upper right corner of your screen.

- Then click on **Edit Name and Photo.**

- Enter your name and choose your profile picture.

- Turn on the switch for **Share Name and Photo,** then select from the three options available for sharing your name and profile picture:

  ✓ Use the **Contacts Only** option to share details with only persons whose numbers you have saved on your smartphone.

  ✓ **Anyone** option gives access to everyone that has your contact details.

  ✓ If you want the system always to prompt you to choose who to share with, then click on the **Always Ask** option. Whenever you open a new message, you will see a pop up on your screen asking for permission to share details with the sender. To share your details, click on **Share** if otherwise, click on **"X"** to refuse and shut down the message.

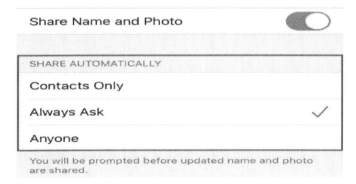

Create and Use Animoji or Memoji

The steps below will show you create a cartoon version of yourself or your loved ones.

- From the settings for name and profile picture, click on the circle for photos close to the name field.
- Then click on the "+" sign to design your own Memoji.

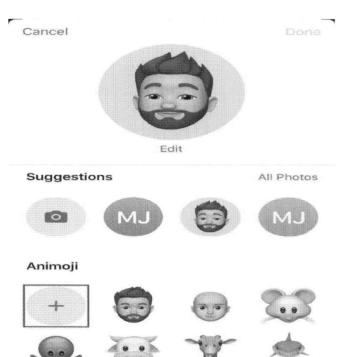

- After you must have created one, click on it to choose a pose for your Memoji and to also use it as your profile picture.

- If you prefer to use a non-personal image, you can select from available Animoji. The Animoji menu selection has several options including sharks and mouse.

- After you must have selected an Animoji or Memoji, scale it, then fit it into the circle.

- Choose a background color to complete your setup.

Customize Your Memoji and Animoji

You can create your own Memoji and Animoji through the steps below:

- Go to **iMessage.**

- Click on a conversation to launch it.

- Click on the Memoji icon.

- Then click on the ⊕ button.

Chapter 15: Email App

Set up Your Device for POP3 Email

- From Settings, go to **Accounts and Password**.
- Click on **Add account**.
- Select your service provider from the list or click on others if your service provider is not on the list.
- Select **Add Mail Account.**
- Input your details, name, email address, and password.
- Under Description, put in your desired name.
- Click on **Next** at the top right corner of the page.
- The next screen is a confirmation that your email has been set up.
- Follow the on-screen instructions to enter any extra information.

Set up Your Device for IMAP Email

- Follow the steps above for POP3, then tap **IMAP.**
- Under hostname, type in the name of your email provider's incoming server.
- Fill in the username and password for your account.
- Under outgoing host server, type in the name of your email provider's outgoing server and tap **Next.**
- Select **Save** at the top right of the screen to save your email address.

Set up Your Device for Exchange Email

- From Settings, go to **Accounts and Password**.

- Click on **Add account**.

- Select **Exchange** under email service provider.

- Input your email address.

- Under Description, put in your desired name.

- Click on **Sign In.**

- Input your email password on the next screen.

- Click on **Sign In.**

- Move the indicator next to the needed data type to enable or disable data synchronization.

- Select **Save** at the top right of the screen to save your email address.

Create a Default Email Account

- From Settings, go to **Mail** at the bottom of the page.

- Click on **Default Account.**

- On the next screen, click on the email address you wish to set as default.

Delete Email Account

- From Settings, go to **Accounts and Password**.

- Click on the email address you want to delete.

- Select **Delete Account** at the bottom of the page.

- On the next screen, click on **Delete from my iPhone.**

Compose and Send Email

- From the Home screen, click on Mail.
- Click on the back arrow at the top left of the screen.
- Select the sending email address.
- Click the new email icon at the bottom right side of the screen.
- On the **To** field, input the receiver email address and the subject of the email.
- Write your email content in the body of the email.
- To insert a video or picture, press and hold the text input field until a pop-up menu comes up on the screen.
- Click **Insert Pictures or Videos** from the pop-up and then follow the instructions you see on the screen to attach the media.
- To attach a document, select **Add Attachment** and follow the instructions you see on the screen.
- Click on **Send** at the top right of the screen.

Block Spam and Unknown Senders

Any email received from blocked senders will be sent straight to the trash folder. Like the "silence unknown callers" feature, you are not blocking the senders as you can always go to the trash folder to see messages sent in there, which is better than preventing the contacts totally from reaching you. At the moment, Apple has a single folder where you will see all blocked spammers and contacts. So, for all the phone numbers you may have blocked in the past either from the Messages app, FaceTime, or Phone, you can find them together with the blocked email addresses. Before this will apply to the mail app, you need to modify your block setting. This setting is what determines what the mail app should do with emails received from blocked contacts.

- From the settings app, click on **Mail.**
- Then go to **Threading.**
- Click on **Blocked Sender,** and you will see three options

- If you enable the option for **None,** it will automatically disable the email blocking feature.
- The option, **"Mark as Blocked, Leave in Inbox,"** means that you will receive emails from your blocked contacts directly in your inbox without being notified.
- The option, **"Move to Trash,"** will send all emails from blocked contacts to the trash folder. You can choose to set the trash folder to delete automatically, or to delete it manually.

95

Note: this feature will apply to all the accounts you have in your mail app, including Outlook, Gmail, Yahoo, etc.

Block a Contact Through Their Emails

Whenever you receive an email from an unknown sender or someone you do not wish to read from again, you can get them blocked right in the mail app.

- Open the email.
- Click on the contact fields at the top of the email to see all the parties in the send list.
- Then click on the email address you want to block.
- On the next screen, you will see an expanded menu option.
- Click on **Block This Contact,** then click on the prompt again to accept your action.
- And that email address is blocked!
- Every email from a blocked contact will also have a notification at the top that says **"This message is from a sender in your blocked list,"** along with a blocked hand icon.

Unblock a Sender Through Received Email

For blocked email addresses, you can unblock by going to the sender's contact details in the email and then click on **"Unblock this Contact."** The hand icon may not instantly disappear, but the sender will be unblocked immediately.

Block a Contact Via Settings App

Another way to block a sender is via the settings app.

- Go to the settings app and click on **Mail.**
- Go down on the page then click on **Blocked.**
- On this screen, you will see all the blocked email addresses and phone numbers.
- Go to the end of the screen and click on **Add New.**
- You will receive a prompt to choose the sender to block.
- The number or email address will immediately appear on the blocked list.

Note: you need to save the contact of the person you wish to block to be able to use this option. If you do not have the email address saved, you may have to block them from the inbox.

Unblock a Contact

- Use the steps above to access the list of blocked contacts.
- Then short swipe from the left side of the email address or phone number you want to unblock.
- After which, you click on **Unblock.**
- Alternatively, you can make a long swipe on the contact to unblock it automatically.
- Another way is to click on **Edit** at the right top of your screen, then click on the ⊖button beside the email address or phone number you want to unblock, then click on **Unblock.**

Chapter 16: Text and Typing

Swipe Typing

The swipe typing feature is now a default feature in the iPhone keyboard. With this feature, you can type on your screen with a swipe of your fingers across the keys of your keyboard instead of clicking on each word. The keyword will deduce the right words you are entering and then insert it into your message. It may seem confusing at first, but once you get familiar with it, you will realize that you type faster with this than when you are tapping on each key. By default, the feature is enabled on your device, and it does not require any further action before you can use it. For instance, if you want to type "friend," tap on the "f" key on your keyboard then swipe your finger over the "r," "I," up till "d" keys in the correct order. The keyboard will automatically pick up the words you wish to type.

However, swipe typing may not be as accurate as regular typing, but this can be corrected. Each time you finish swiping, you will see three options on your keyboard for the words swiped. Click on the right one. If the keyboard entered the right word, rather than clicking, you can continue to swipe your next words for the system to select it automatically. The keyboard has been designed to get better the more you make use of the feature, but when dealing with uncommon words, it is advisable to begin by tap typing first.

Disable Swipe Typing

If you find this feature hard to use or annoying, you can use the steps below to disable it.

- Go to the settings app.

- Click on **General.**

- Then select **Keyboards.**

- Navigate to **Slide to Type** and move the switch to the left to disable the option.

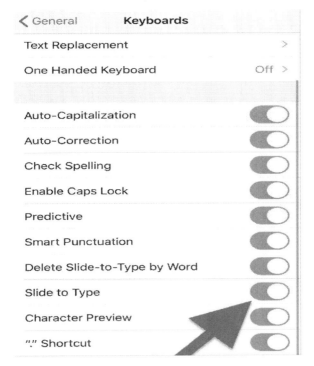

You can also disable the feature using the keyboard.

- Long press on the keyboard switcher.

- Then click on **Keyboard Settings.**
- Depending on your keyboard setup, you will see the switcher as a Globe icon or an Emoji icon.
- Navigate to **"Slide to Type"** and move the switch to the left to disable the option.

Note: To disable with the keyboard method, you need to have more than one keyboard activated on your device.

Use the New Gestures for Copy, Cut, Paste, Redo and Undo

For most of us, we use the iPhone as our primary way of communicating with people. While the "shake to undo" gesture is still available, Apple has now added a 3-finger gesture to make it easy for typing.

Copy, Cut and Paste

To get the best results on this feature, I will advise that you use your two fingers and thumb for this function.

- To copy, use your three fingers to pinch on the text and then un-pinch (expand your fingers) using your three fingers to Paste the text you copied.
- Perform the copy gesture twice with your finger to cut out the text. While the first gesture will copy the text, the second gesture will cut out the text.
- If you look at the top of your screen, you will see the badges for "Copy," "Cut," or "Paste" to verify your action.

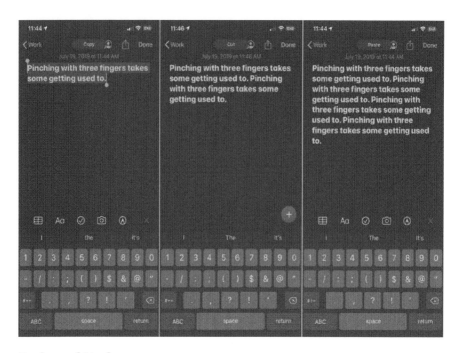

Redo and Undo

- To undo, swipe to the left with your three fingers on the screen.

- Another way to undo is by double-clicking on the screen with your three fingers.

- To Redo, swipe to the right with your three fingers on the screen.

- If you look at the top of your screen, you will see the badges for "Redo" or "Undo" to verify your action.

Access the Shortcut Bar

If you will rather not make use of the gestures, you can go for the shortcut bar. Regardless of the part of the screen you are on, including the keyboard area, click and hold on the screen with your three fingers for approximately a second to launch the shortcut bar. You will see the bar at the top of your screen with buttons for **Cut, Undo, Copy, Redo and Paste.** The bar will remain as you repeat the command, but as soon as you enter text or move your cursor, the bar disappears.

Chapter 17: Manage Applications and Data

Install Apps from the App Store

- Open the app store and click on search.

- Type the name of the app into the search field.

- Click on **Search**.

- Select the desired app.

- Click on **GET** beside the app and follow the steps on the screen to install the app. For paid apps, click on the price to install.

Uninstall Apps

To delete third-party apps installed on your phone,

- Long-press on an app on your home screen until the apps begin to jiggle. You will see an **X mark** beside each app icon.

- Click on the **X** icon at the top of the app you want to uninstall.

Move Between Apps

Switching Apps can be tricky without a home button, but the below steps will make it as seamless as possible.

- To open the App Switcher, swipe up from the bottom of the screen and then wait for a second.
- Release your finger once the app thumbnails appear.
- To flip through open apps, swipe either left or right, and select the app you want.

Force Close Apps in the iPhone

You do this mostly when an app isn't responding.

- Merely swiping up from the bottom of the screen will show the app switcher. This will display all the open apps in card-like views.
- To force close the app, locate the app from the app switcher and swipe up to close the app.
- Tap on the minus button for each of the apps you wish to close.
- To go through apps used in the past, swipe horizontally at the bottom of your home screen.

Delete Apps

The steps below will show you delete apps fast.

- Click and hold the app until it begins to shake.
- Click on **Delete** app, then select **Delete.**

Delete Apps From the App Store

- Open the app store.

- You will see your account picture at the right top corner of your screen, click on it.

- Go to the section for **Updated Recently**

- If you wish to delete any recently updated app, make a swipe gesture to the left on the particular app you want to remove.

- Then click on the red button that will appear on your screen.

Delete Apps from the Update Screen

This is yet another way to delete apps you no longer want.

- From the app store, you will notice that the update for apps is now under the **Account card.** (click on your picture at the right top of your screen)

- If you see any app you wish to delete from the displayed list, make a swipe gesture to the left on that particular app, and you will see the option to delete the app.

- You can use this step for all the apps you see in the list whether the app has been updated or is pending update.

Delete Apps Without Losing App Data

- From the **Settings** app, click on **General.**

- Click on **iPhone Storage.**

- Click on the app you wish to uninstall and click on **Offload App.**

- Select **Offload App** again to complete.

Control Automatic App Update

- Open the **Settings** app, and click on the banner that has your name and your profile picture at the top of the screen.

- Click on **iTunes and App Store.**

- Besides the **App Update** option, move the switch left or right to enable or disable the option.

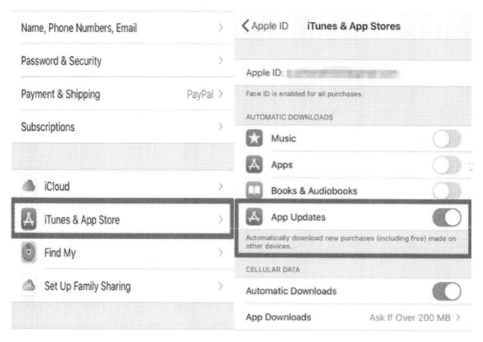

Modify Settings for Background App Refresh

When you move to a different app, some apps continue to run before they are suspended. The Background App Refresh allows suspended apps to check for new content and updates. Follow the steps below to enable or disable this feature:

- From the **Settings** app, go to **General.**
- Click on **Background App Refresh.**
- Then click on **Background App Refresh** again.
- Select **OFF** to disable or **ON** to enable.
- To refresh the apps using Wi-fi, select **Wi-fi.**
- Select **Wi-fi and Mobile Data** if you want the system to refresh using either wi-fi or mobile data.
- Use the back button to return to the previous screen.
- Toggle on or off the button for each app to enable or disable.

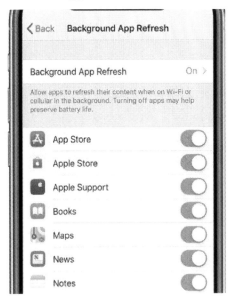

Configure Your iPhone For Manual Syncing

- Using either Wi-fi or USB, connect your iPhone to a computer.
- Manually open the iTunes app if it doesn't come up automatically.
- Tap on the iPhone icon on the top left side of the screen. If you have multiple iDevices, rather than seeing the iPhone icon, you will see a menu showing all the connected iDevices. Once the devices are displayed, select your current device.
- Tap on the **Apply** button at the bottom right corner of your screen.
- Tap on the Sync button if it doesn't start syncing automatically.

Use Cycle Tracking in Health

The health app allows you to do lots of things beneficial to your health, like the menstrual cycle tracking as well as tools to know your most fertile days and your due date.

- Launch the health app.
- Click on **Search** and select **Cycle Tracking** from the displayed list.
- Click on **Get started**, then click on **Next.**
- The app will request a series of information like the duration of your period and the date the last one started.
- You also get to choose how you will like to track your period as well as confirm if you want to receive notifications and predictions on your next possible cycle.

- Confirm if you want to be able to record spotting and symptoms in your cycle log as well as if you wish to have access to your fertility windows.
- After you have provided all the responses, you can then go back to the **Cycle Tracking** homepage.
- In the **Cycle Tracking** homepage, click on **Add Period** to input days of your last periods.
- You can also click on **Spotting, Symptoms,** and **Flow Levels** option to input more specific details.

Share Music Over Two AirPods

The steps below will show you share music over two AirPods.

- Connect the first AirPods to your iPhone then position the second AirPod case beside the iPhone.
- Click on the **Round button** located at the back of the Airpods.
- Then click on **Connect.**

- After you have successfully paired the second device with your iPhone, you will now see it as an option on the screen for Airplay.
- To select the second pair, click on the name.
- The audio will immediately go through the two Airpods in sync.

Use Music Player

- Click on the **Music Player** icon on the home screen.
- Click on **Playlist** then click on **New Playlist.**
- Tap the text box that has **Description,** type in the name for that playlist.
- Click on **Add Music.**
- Go to the category and click on the audio file you want to add.
- Select **Done** at the top of the screen.
- Select **Done** again.
- Go to the playlist and click on the music.
- Use the Volume key to control the volume.
- Click on the song title.
- Tap the right arrow to go to the next music or the left arrow to go to the previous music.
- Gently slide your finger up the screen.
- Click on shuffle to set it on or off.
- Click on **Repeat** to set it on or off. You can choose as many kinds of music as you want to be on **Repeat.**

Save Your Passwords

Each time you log in to an app or service, you will receive a prompt to save your password to the iCloud keychain. You can also manage your details manually with the steps below.

- Go to the settings app and click on **Passwords & Accounts.**

- Then click on **Website & App Passwords.**

- The system may prompt you to use your passcode, or Touch ID before granting you access.

Sign in With Apple

Not so many of us are comfortable with using our Instagram login details to sign in to several apps. This feature allows you to sign in to apps without inputting your personal information. You will see the **Sign In With Apple** option displayed on the opening screen of compatible apps.

- Click on the option for **"Sign in with Apple,"** you will get a prompt to log in to your Apple account.

- On the next screen, choose only the information you want the app developer to access.

- This feature allows you to decide to share your email address or not to share it.

- If you choose not to share your email, Apple gives you a random email address that will be linked to your Apple iCloud email address. Any email sent to this random address will be automatically forwarded to your registered email address.

Chapter 18: The New Reminders App

The Reminders app has several modifications and additions. Before now, the app lacked some features that are in similar third party apps. In the steps below, you will learn explore and use the revamped reminders app.

Create a Reminder

- Launch the reminders app.
- Then click on **reminders** under **My List** heading
- Then select **New Reminders** at the bottom of your screen, on the left side.

- Fill in your details for the reminder.

- Then click **Return** on your keyboard to confirm your first reminder.

Add a New Task

From the home screen of the reminder app, you can now see all the reminders you have at the moment, those due today as well as numbers contained in each list. If you want to add a new task to an existing list, follow the steps below:

- From the home screen of the reminder app, click on **All.**
- Then click the ⊕ button located underneath each category to add a new task

The app now allows you to add time or date, change the category for a task, or set up a reminder for the task when in a specified location. To achieve this, click on the desired tasks to launch the options, then click on the ⓘ icon and set as desired.

Add SubTasks

For projects or tasks that are complex or have several levels, you can add sub-tasks or create a multi-entry list. The steps below will guide you to create subtasks.

- Go to the desired task on your reminder app.
- Then click on the ⓘ icon at the top right side of your screen to see the available options.
- Go down on the next screen and click on **Subtasks.**
- Then click on **Add Reminder** to include a subtask.
- You can add as many subtasks as you want in a single task.

- You can locate the subtask in the reminder app or click on the main task.

- You may complete the subtasks without completing the parent task.

- You can also click on the ⓘ icon at the top right of your screen to add time, location, or contacts for each subtask.

Create a List

You can group all your tasks into a single list to make room on your reminder app's home page.

- Open the reminders app.

- Navigate to the right bottom of your screen and then click on **Add list.**

- You will see varieties of logos and colors to choose from to help you identify each list at a glance.

- Click on **Done** at the right top side of your screen.

- To add reminders or tasks to this list, click on the list under **My List**, tap the ⓘ icon, then choose the reminder/ task that you want to add to the list.

- To add an existing task to a list, open the task, then click on the ⓘicon at the top of your screen. Click on **List** then click on the desired list.

Note: to quickly find a task, you can search using the search bar option.

Add a List to a Group

You can add all the lists that fall in the same category into a general group. Say you have one list for anniversaries and another for birthdays, you can have a group titled "memorable dates" and then move the lists into this group to make your home page look more appealing.

- From the homepage of the reminder app, click on **Edit** at the right top corner of your screen.

- Then click on **Add Group** at the bottom left of your screen.

- Type the name you want for the group and then select the lists that should go into that group.

- Click on **Done.**

- To modify the lists in each group, click on **Edit** again.

- Then click on the ⓘicon.

- With the *Include* option, you can remove or add lists.

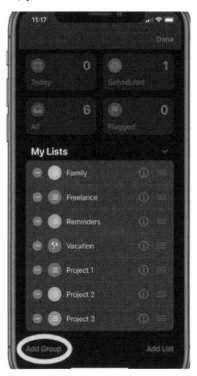

Add Location, Time or a Connected person

Now, you do not have to manually go through your list as you can add a time or location to a set reminder, and your phone will prod you at the arranged time or place. After setting your reminder, use the ⓘicon at the right side of your task to access the task options.

- If you want to be reminded at a particular location, select *Remind me at a* **location** and then choose your desired location.

- If you wish to be reminded at a fixed time, go to **Remind me on a day,** enable the option, and then fill in required details for "**Alarm or Reminds me at a time."**

- For repeating tasks, choose the option for **Repeat.**

- If the reminder has to do with a contact, you can design the task to alert you when next you message the contact. To do this, click on **Remind me when messaging** *and then choose your preferred contact.*

Today Notification Feature

By default, the reminders app notifies you of your tasks for the day, but you can choose not to receive any notification or the best time to be notified. Follow the steps below:

- From the settings app, click on **Reminders.**
- You can choose to turn off notifications entirely or change the timing for the notification under **Today Notification.**
- You can also modify your tasks' default list while on this screen.

Use Siri as a Reminder

Siri can do a lot of things, which include asking the virtual assistant to remind you of a task. You can say to Siri, "remind me to," followed by the information. If you want Siri to tell you at a specific place or time, ask.

Chapter 19: Find My

The Find My iPhone and Find My Friends apps were collapsed into a single app called **"Find My."** This new app allows you to find your missing devices as well as share your location with your loved ones.

Share Your Location

- Open the **Find My** app on your home screen.

- Navigate to the **People** tab to see your current location.

- To send your location, click on **Start Sharing Location.**

- Type the name of the contact you want to send your location.

Find Missing Device

- Go to the tab for **Devices** to see all the registered Apple devices.

- Select the missing device, and you will see the following options on your screen: **Mark As Lost, Get Directions** to the device, remotely *Erase This Device, or Play Sound.* Select the option that bests suit your needs.

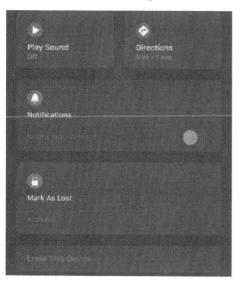

- If the device is not connected to the internet at the time this action was performed, you can choose to receive a notification once the device comes online. To do this, click the **Notify Me** option

Choose Settings for Find My

- Click on your Apple ID in the Settings app.
- Scroll down and click on **Find My.**
- Enable or disable **Find My iPhone.**
- Turn on **Enable Offline Finding** if you want to see your phone even when it is offline.
- Turn on **Send Last Location** to send your device location to Apple once the battery is low.

Chapter 20: Apple Map

Use the Look Around Feature in Apple Maps

If you are familiar with the Streetview from Google, you can relate to Apple's Look Around Feature. This feature allows you to preview a particular location before you physically visit. The steps below will guide you on use this feature.

- Type your desired location in the Apple Map's search bar.
- Then press long on the map to select this location.
- Every location that supports the **Look Around** feature will show a **look around** image on the screen.
- Click on the **Look Around** image to go to the street level and then drag to look around the location.
- This screen also shows you facts about the location, and you can swipe up from the bottom of your screen to add the area to your favorites list.

Use Favorites in the Apple Maps

iOS 13 brought several improvements to Apple map, including beaches, roads, buildings, and other exciting details. Some other cool features were added recently, like being able to add a location to your list of Favorites. Another exciting feature is the ability to organize all your saved places in a personal customized collection. Follow the steps below to add a favorite on the map.

- Manually search for a location by inputting the address or click on the desired location.

- Navigate to the bottom of your screen and click on **Add to Favorites.**

- Whenever you want to view your favorites list, go to the home screen of the map app.

Begin a New Collection

To begin a new collection,

- Go to the home page of the Apple map.

- Swipe from the bottom of the screen upwards.

- Then click on **New Collections** to make a new list.

To add a particular location to your customized collection,

- Drag up from the Apple maps' main page and click on **My Places.**

- Select **Add a Place.**

- On the next screen, add all your recently viewed location to your collection or use the search bar to find a particular area and add to the group.

Chapter 21: Gaming

You can now take your gaming experience to the next level by playing games on your iPhone with the DualShock 4 or the Xbox One Controller.

Pair your iPhone with an Xbox One S controller

- From the settings app, click on **Bluetooth** to enable the Bluetooth menu.
- The **Xbox One** controller has to be 100% charged.
- Press the Xbox logo button to power it on.
- Go to the back of the controller and press the wireless enrollment button there. Hold down the button for some seconds.
- Please skip this step if you have already unpaired the controller from a different device. You can press and hold the Xbox button to put it in pairing mode.
- If you haven't unpaired before, continue with the steps below.
- The Xbox button light will begin to flash quickly.
- Go to your Bluetooth menu on your smartphone and locate the **"Xbox Wireless Controller"** from the list, then click on it.
- Once the light stops blinking and remains focused, then you know that pairing is complete.

Disconnect Xbox One Controller from your iPhone

To disconnect using the controller, hold down the Xbox button for approximately 10 seconds. If you will rather disconnect via the iPhone, it is best to go through the control center.

- swipe from the bottom of your screen up.
- Hold down the Bluetooth icon on your screen.
- When you see a pop-up menu on your screen, press down on **Bluetooth: On.**
- Then on the next pop up, you will see the name "Xbox Wireless Controller" showing on the list.
- Click on the controller to completely disconnect from your device.

You can also go through another step shown below:

- From the settings app, click on **Bluetooth.**
- From the pop-up on your screen, press down on **Bluetooth: On.**
- Then on the next pop up, you will see the name "Xbox Wireless Controller" showing on the list.
- Click on the controller to completely disconnect from your device.

There is yet another method, as shown below:

- From the settings app, click on **Bluetooth.**
- Then go to the list for **My Devices,** you will find "Xbox Wireless Controller."
- Besides the controller option to the right, click on ⓘ.
- From the next pop-up, click on **Disconnect.**
- Just press the Xbox button when next you want to use the controller on your iPhone.

Unpair the Xbox Controller from your iPhone

Follow the steps above to disconnect the devices but rather than clicking on **Disconnect,** click on **"Forget This Device."**

Pair your iPhone with a DualShock 4

The DualShock 4 controller should be fully charged before you proceed with the steps below:

- From the settings app, click on **Bluetooth** to enable the Bluetooth menu.

- Press both the Share and PlayStation Button ⏺ of the controller at the same time and hold down for a few seconds.

- You should see lights begin to flash intermittently at the back of the controller.

- Go to the Bluetooth menu on your iPhone, and you will find the **DualShock 4 Wireless controller** as one of the devices on the displayed list. Click on the controller.

- Once the blinking light at the back of the controller changes to reddish-pink color, it means that the devices have paired.

Disconnect a DualShock 4 from your iPhone

Whenever you are not making use of the controller, I will advise you to turn off the Bluetooth connection. If you rather go through the controller, hold down the PlayStation button for approximately 10 seconds. You can also use the steps below to disconnect directly on your iPhone.

- Swipe up from the bottom of your screen.

- Hold down the Bluetooth icon on your screen.
- When you see a pop-up menu on your screen, press down on **Bluetooth: On.**
- Then on the next pop up, you will see the name "DUALSHOCK 4 Wireless Controller" showing on the list.
- Click on the controller to completely disconnect from your device.

You can also go through another step shown below:

- From the settings app, click on **Bluetooth.**
- From the pop-up on your screen, press down on **Bluetooth: On.**
- Then on the next pop up, you will see the name "DUALSHOCK 4 Wireless Controller" showing on the list.
- Click on the controller to completely disconnect from your device.

There is yet another method, as shown below:

- From the settings app, click on **Bluetooth.**
- Then go to the list for **My Devices,** you will find "DUALSHOCK 4 Wireless Controller."
- Besides the controller option to the right, click on ⓘ.
- From the next pop-up, click on **Disconnect.**

After the first successful pairing of the controller to your iPhone, when next you want to play with the controller, you need to press the PlayStation button with Bluetooth enabled on your iPhone for both devices to pair.

Unpair the DualShock 4 from your iPhone

To unpair, follow the steps above to disconnect the devices. Then click on **Forget This Device,** and not **Disconnect.**

Chapter 22: Screenshots

Take a Screenshot

Without the home button, taking a snapshot may seem tricky; however, follow these steps to help you make the best shots possible.

- Press both the side and the Volume Up button simultaneously to take a screenshot.
- Screenshots are saved automatically in the Photos app, under the **Screenshots** album.

View Screenshots

Here is how to view screenshots on your phone

- go to **Photos,** click on **Albums,** go to **Media Types,** and select **Screenshots.**
- To edit the image, click on the image and tap the thumbnail at the left bottom corner of your iPhone.

Save Screenshots in the Files App on Your iPhone

You can choose to save your screenshots in the Files app instead of the Photos app. The steps below will show you achieve this.

- After taking your screenshot, click on the little preview in the Markup to view and edit it.
- Click on **Done.**
- Click on **Save to Files** to save the screenshots in the Files app or your preferred location other than the Photos app.

Scan Documents Straight to Files App

Your phone has an in-built scanner that you can use for scanning your documents. You also have the option of choosing where the scanned files should be stored.

- Go to the Files app.

- Click on at the top right side of your screen.

- Click on **Scan Document** from the pop-up list.

- The camera will search for a document in the viewfinder and automatically capture the document. If you do not want to use the automatic settings, click on **Auto** at the top right side of the camera screen, then select **Manual** setting.

- Click on the icon at the top of the screen to select a color for your document.
- Focus your phone camera on the document you want to scan, then click on the shutter button to scan the document.

Keep Track of Documents

On your iPhone, you can access folders and files stored on your iCloud Drive and any other cloud storage services. You can also access and restore folders and files deleted from your device within the last 30 days. There are three subsections in the Browse tab, and they are:

1. **Locations**: To view files saved in iCloud, click on **iCloud Drive**. To view files recently deleted from your device, click on **Recently Deleted.**

   To add an external cloud storage service, you need to first install the app from the App Store (Google Drive, Dropbox, etc.), then click **Edit** at the right top corner of your device screen to activate it. Once done, click on **Done.**

   Other available options for folders and files are:

   - To view the content of a folder, click on the folder.
   - To Copy, Rename, Duplicate, Delete, Move, Tag, Share or Get info of a folder or file, press the folder, or file for some seconds.
   - To download items with the cloud and arrow icon, tap on them.

- To annotate a file, click on the pencil tip icon at the right upper side of the screen. It is essential to know that this feature is only available to select image file formats and PDF.

2. **Favorites:** To add folders to the Favorite section, press the folder for some seconds until a menu pops up, then select **Favorite** from the list. Currently, you can only do this from the iCloud Device, and only for folders, no single files.

3. **Tags:** when using macros Finder tags, you will see them in the Tags section. Alternatively, press a file for some seconds to tag such a file. Then click **"A Tag Here"** to see all the files that have that tag.

Chapter 23: Safari

Safari is the default browser available on all Apple devices, including the iPhone.

Access Website Settings for Safari

The Safari browser witnessed several additions and upgrades with the iOS 13. One of these changes is the ability to customize different settings for different websites. Similar to how it works on the Safari browser for your Mac device, you are now able to modify security and viewing options differently for each website settings. Safari then applies the settings so that you do not have to run them repeatedly. The steps below will show you achieve this.

- Visit a site that you use regularly.

- Tap on the "aA" icon at the left top corner of your screen to show the **View menu** of the website.

- Select **Website settings.**

- You will see three options displayed, as shown below:
- ✓ **Request Desktop Website:** click on this to view desktop versions of a website on your mobile device.
- ✓ **Reader Mode** option helps to make online articles more readable by removing extraneous web page contents from it. Click on **"Use Reader Automatically"** to activate this feature by default.
- ✓ **Camera, Microphone, Location:** these last three options allow you to choose if you want sites to have access to your microphone, camera as well as if the sites should be able to access your location. You can choose either **Deny** or **Allow.** Click on **Ask** to give permission per time. This way, whenever sites wish to access these features, Safari will first seek your consent.

Access Safari Download Manager

The download manager shows you a list of items that are downloading and ones that were downloaded previously. When you attempt to download a file, a little download icon will appear at the right top corner of your screen. When you click on this icon, you will see how far the download has gone. Click on the magnifying glass beside the downloaded file to go straight to the folder where the file is stored, whether in the cloud or on your phone's local storage.

Auto-Close Open Tabs in Safari

For several users, when you launch the Safari browser, you will find several open tabs from social media posts to Quora to Google searches. For most of these opened tabs, you may not go back to them, but it could be quite bothersome to close each tab individually. The good news is that there is now a feature that can automatically close open tabs in the Safari browser after a defined time. The steps below will show you how to manage the option.

- From the settings app, click on **Safari.**

- Click on **Tabs** then click on **Close Tabs.**
- The next screen will show a timeline for open tabs to close. The default option is **"Manually."**
- You can pick from the other options if you desire: **After One Week, After One Day** or **After One Month.**

- Choose the option that will best suit your need.

Choose When Downloaded File List is Cleared

Safari on the iPhone has a download manager similar to what we have on Mac. By default, the downloaded file list clears at the end of each day. But, you can change this setting to manually clear the list or to clear the list once the download is complete.

- From the Settings app, click on **Safari.**

- Click on **Downloads.**

- Select **Remove Download List Items**.

- Make your pick from the three available options on your screen: **Upon successful download, After one day,** or **Manually.**

Modify Where Downloaded Files from Safari are Saved

By default, all downloaded files are saved in the **Download folder** of the Files app, but you can modify this by selecting an alternative storage location with the steps below:

- Go to the Settings app.

- Click on **Safari.**

- Then click on **Downloads.**

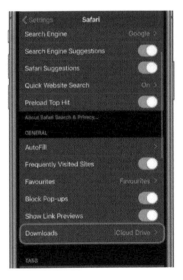

- You can then make your choice from the available options: On My iPhone, iCloud Drive, or in another location that you want.

Enable Content Blockers in Safari

- From the Settings app, click on **Safari.**

- Then click on **Content Blockers.**

- To enable this option, move the switch beside it to the right.

Note: You need to have at least one 3rd party content blocker installed on your phone.

Temporarily Disable Content Blockers in Safari

Some sites require you to disable content blockers before you can access them. For sites like this, you can temporarily disable the content blocker.

- From the Safari browser, go to any website of choice.
- Click on the "aA" icon at the left top corner of your screen to show the View menu of that site.

- Then click on **Turn Off Content Blockers.**
- To disable this feature for just one website, click on **Website Settings** and then move the switch beside **Use Content Blockers** to the left to disable it.

Share or Save a Safari Web Page as a PDF

You can save a webpage as a PDF document with the steps below:

- Launch the Safari browser then go to the webpage you want to save as PDF.

- Press both the Side button and the Volume Up button at the same time to take a screenshot.
- A preview of the screenshot will show at the left lower side of the screen.
- When you click on the preview, it will open the **Instant Markup Interface.** You need to be fast with this as you have only 5 secs before this screen disappears.
- Click on **Full-Page** in the right upper corner of the Markup interface.
- Then click on **Done** and select **Save PDF to Files** to save as PDF.
- Click on the **Share** button to share the PDF and choose who and how you want to share it.

List of New Keyboard Shortcuts

During the WWDC conference, Apple noted that they included about 30 new shortcuts in Safari, which has been compiled below for your reference.

- For the default font size in Reader (Cmd + 0)
- Increase Reader text size (Cmd + +)
- Decrease Reader text size (Cmd + -)
- Actual size (Cmd + 0)
- Toggle downloads (Cmd + Alt)
- Open link in background (Cmd + tap)
- Open link in new tab (Cmd + Shift + tap)
- Open link in new window (Cmd + Alt + tap)

- New Private tab (Cmd + Shift + N)
- Close other tabs (Cmd + Alt + W)
- Save webpage (Cmd + S)
- Zoom out (Cmd + -)
- Email this page (Cmd + I)
- Use selection for Find (Cmd + E)
- Zoom in (Cmd + +)
- Focus Smart Search field (Cmd + Alt + F)
- Close web view in app (Cmd + W)
- Change focused element (Alt + tab)
- To download linked file (Alt + tap)
- Add link to your Reading List (Shift + tap)
- Paste without formatting content (Cmd + Shift + Alt + V)
- To toggle bookmarks (Cmd + Alt + 1)
- Navigate around screen (arrow keys)
- Open search result (Cmd + Return)

Chapter 24: Wifi and Connectivity

Join a Wi-fi Network

- Go to Settings, then click on Wi-fi.
- Move the switch beside **Wi-fi** to the right to put on the Wi-fi.
- Select your Wi-fi network from the drop-down.
- Type in the password and click on **Join.**

Control Wi-fi Setup

- From the top right side of the screen, draw down the screen.
- Click on the Wi-fi icon to enable or disable.
- Move the switch beside **Wi-fi** to the right or left to put off or on.

Control Mobile Data

- Go to **Mobile Data** under **Settings**.
- Move the switch beside **Mobile Data** to the right or left to put off or on.
- Scroll to where you have the applications and move the switch beside each app to the right or left to put off or on.

Control Data Roaming

- Go to **Mobile Data** under **Settings**.
- Click on **Mobile Data Options.**
- Move the switch beside **Data Roaming** to the right or left to put off or on.

Use Your iPhone as a Hotspot

- Go to **Personal Hotspot** under **Settings**.

- Move the switch beside **Personal Hotspot** to the right or left to put off or on.
- IF wi-fi is disabled, click **Turn on Wi-fi and Bluetooth.**
- Select **Wi-fi and USB only** if wi-fi is enabled already.
- Input the wi-fi password beside the field for a wi-fi password.
- Select **Done** at the top of the screen.

Control Automatic Use of Mobile Data
- Go to **Mobile Data** under **Settings.**
- Move the switch beside **Wi-fi Assist** to the right or left to put off or on.

Download Large Apps over Cellular Network
When downloading apps above 200MB, you will see a popup to confirm if you want to continue the download using cellular data, or you will download it **"Later on Wi-Fi."** But you have to enable this feature first.

- From the settings app, click on **iTunes & App Store.**
- On the next screen, click on the appropriate option.

✓ **Always Allow** will complete your download without any further confirmation.

✓ **Ask If Over 200MB** if you want to choose either Wi-fi or cellular.

✓ **Ask First** will require your confirmation before any download over 200MB.

Chapter 25: Battery Tips

The iPhone battery tends to run down fast because of the different functions that the iPhone offer. I have compiled a list of things you can do to save your battery life. You do not need to perform all the tips stated here, pick a few that you are okay with.

Set Optimized Battery Charging

Optimized Battery Charging helps to reduce wear on your phone battery and also improve the battery lifespan by reducing the time your smartphone spends fully charged. With this feature enabled, your device will stop charging past 80% in most cases. The processor is designed to activate this feature only when it predicts that the phone will be connected to a charger for a long time.

- From the Settings app on your smartphone, click on **Battery.**
- Click on **Battery Health.**

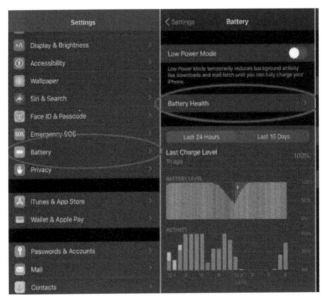

- On the next screen, you will see data showing the maximum battery capacity for your phone battery, an indication of the level of degradation, and the option to enable **Optimized Battery Charging**.

- Navigate to **Optimized Battery Charging** and move the switch to the right to enable this feature.

Stop Background Apps Refresh

One feature built to make your iPhone not only smart but also ready for you to use when needed is the Background App Refresh. The work of this feature is to look out for apps that you use often and the period in the day that you use these apps and then carry out automatic updates on the app so that you can have the latest information the next time you launch these apps. Follow the steps below to disable this feature on your smartphone.

- Go to the settings app and click on **General.**
- Then click on **Background App Refresh.**

- Move the slider to the left to disable this feature for the whole apps or disable the feature for select apps.

Disable Auto Update of Apps

You may have set up the option to automatically update your apps as soon as there is a new version, and this can drain the battery life. Follow the steps below to disable this feature and manually update your apps.

- From the settings app, click on the **iTunes & App Store**.
- Click on the button beside **App Updates** to disable the auto app update feature.

Extend the Device Battery Life

Some apps and services on the iPhone draw lots of power, which will drain the battery life faster. You can turn on low power mode to reduce power consumption.

- From **Settings**, go to **Battery**.
- Move the switch beside **Low Power Mode** to the right to enable.

Disable Auto App Suggestions

This feature makes use of your location service to discover your area and suggest apps that you may need based on your location. While it is a cool feature, it can, however, drain the battery. The steps below will show you disable the feature.

- Open the Settings app and click on **Siri & Search**.

- Under **Siri Suggestion,** toggle off **Suggestions in Search** and **Suggestions in Look Up.**

- You may also toggle off **Suggestions on Lock Screen.**

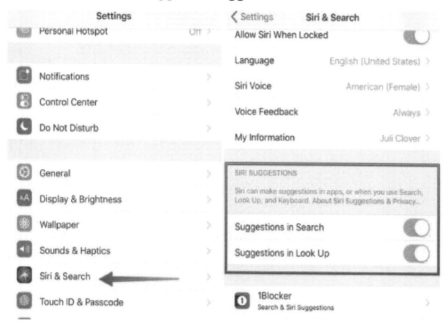

Enable Auto-Brightness

The auto-brightness feature makes your phone to adjust its brightness based on the lighting condition per time. The feature will save you battery life as it controls the energy used on the phone.

- From the Settings app, click on **Accessibility.**

- Then click on **Display & Text Size**.

- Scroll down and toggle off **Auto-Brightness**.

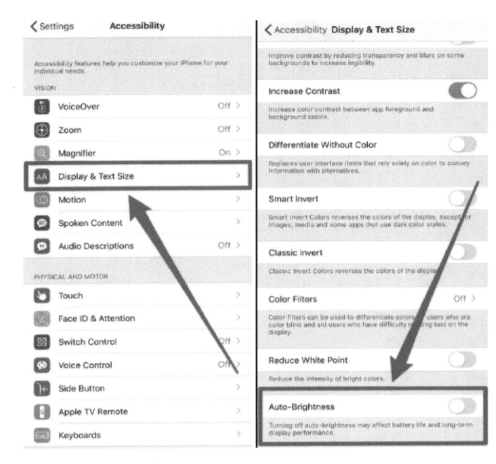

Reduce Screen Brightness

The brighter your screen is, the more power it consumes. You can control your phone's brightness using the slider on your iPhone. When you need to save battery, ensure that the brightness of the screen is at its lowest.

- From the settings app, click on **Display & Brightness**
- Then use the slider to reduce the brightness by pulling to the left.

Stop Motion and Animations

Although this feature is cool, however, disabling it will help to save battery life.

- From the settings app, click on **General.**
- Then click on **Accessibility.**
- Select **Reduce Motion**.
- Move the slider beside **Reduce Motion** to enable it.

Disable Wi-Fi When Not in Use

When not using the Wi-Fi connection, it is advisable to disable it, so it does not drain your battery.

- From the settings app, click on **Wi-Fi.**
- Then move the slider beside **Wi-Fi** to disable it.

You can also disable **Wi-Fi** through the control center. Go to the control center and click on the **Wi-Fi** button until it turns grey.

Locate the Battery Draining Apps

You can find apps using a significant percentage of your battery through a feature called **Battery Usage.** Follow the steps below to use this step

- From Settings app, click on **Battery**
- The apps will be displayed according to the battery usage.
- At times, there may be notes under each app to show reasons the app consumed so much battery and fix it.

Ensure that Personal Hotspot is Disabled

When the hotspot is on, your iPhone becomes a hotspot that shares its cellular data with other devices in range. While it can be useful, it can also drain your battery. Whenever you are done with the hotspot, remember to disable it.

- Go to the Settings app.
- Click on **Personal Hotspot**
- Disable the option using the button beside it.

Disable Bluetooth

Bluetooth is another function that transmits data wirelessly and drains battery while doing so. To save your battery life, then I will advise that you put on Bluetooth only when needed. To either disable or enable your device Bluetooth, go to settings, and click on **Bluetooth.**

Disable Location Services

The iPhone comes with a built-in GPS, which is quite helpful for locating nearby restaurants, stores, etc. as well as finding directions. This app needs to send data over a network that usually tells on the battery of your device. Whenever you are not making use of the location services, you can disable it with the steps below:

- Go to the Settings app.
- Click on **Privacy.**
- Then select **Location Services.**

- Toggle off **Location Services** and then click on **Turn Off** to disable the option.
- Alternatively, you can navigate down the screen to select apps that should not have access to location services.

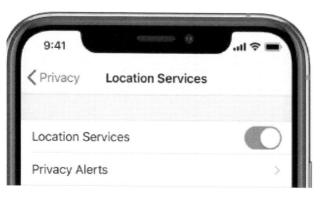

Disable Cellular Data

Similar to the Bluetooth, when using 4G, 5G, LTE, and other cellular connections that have fast transfer speeds, they tend to drain your phone battery. They even consume more power when you are using it heavily, like when making HD calls or streaming videos. I know that the cellular data is essential, which is why you should disable it only when you need to save battery life.

- From the settings app, click on **Cellular.**
- Go to **Cellular Data** and move the switch to the left to disable.

Note: Turning off cellular data will not affect your Wi-Fi connection.

Disable Data Push

You may have configured the email settings to automatically download messages to your smartphone as soon as they get to the email server. It is crucial to be current on your email folder; however, when you continuously download like this, it can drain your battery faster. Rather than the automatic update, you can go to the Mail app and manually refresh the app to receive new messages. The steps below will show you disable the data push feature:

- From the settings app, click on **Passwords & Accounts.**
- Or go to **Mails** from the settings app and click on **Accounts.**
- Then click on **Fetch New Data.**
- Go to **Push** and move the switch to the left to disable.

Set Emails to Download on Schedule

If you do not want to refresh your email manually, you can schedule the emails to download at a specified time. This is a balance between the two steps above, while you will not have to refresh your mail app manually, you will also not get an instant update. This method will still help to achieve the end goal, which is to save battery life.

- From the Settings app, click on **Passwords & Accounts.**
- Then click on **Fetch New Data.**
- Navigate to the bottom and choose your options. The longer the time between checks, the longer your battery life is preserved.

Set up the Screen to Auto-Lock Sooner

Auto-locking your screen helps to save your battery life. As long as your phone has something it is displaying, it will be taking out of the battery life. While I will advise that you select any of the options that suit you, do not choose **Never** as that will drain your battery life.

- From the settings app, click on **Display & Brightness**.

- Then click on **Auto-Lock**.

- Select any of the options from 30 seconds to 5 minutes.

Disable Fitness Tracking

The fitness tracking feature on the iPhone is used to track your steps as well as other fitness activities. It is very beneficial, especially when you are trying to get into shape, but this app also drains the battery. You can disable the feature whenever you are not using it.

- From the settings app, click on **Privacy.**

- Then select **Motion & Fitness**.

- Move the switch beside **Fitness Tracking** to the left to disable this feature.

Disable AirDrop When Not in Use

AirDrop is the wireless file sharing feature of the Apple devices. To use Airdrop, you need to enable both Bluetooth and Wi-Fi and prepare your phone to locate other airdrop enabled devices. This makes use of more battery, and it is advisable to disable when not in use.

- Go to the control center, then click on **AirDrop.**
- Click on **Receiving Off** to disable the feature.
- You can also go to the settings app, click on **General,** select **AirDrop** and change **Receiving Off** or **Contacts Only.**

Disable Automatic Upload of Photos to iCloud

The photo app is set to upload your photos to your device's iCloud account automatically. Disable the auto-uploads and attempt to upload only when you have a full battery or when moving from your computer. Follow the steps below to check if your photos are always uploaded to iCloud.

- Go to the settings app.
- Click on **Photos.**
- Then click on **iCloud Photos**

Stop Sending Diagnostic Data to Developers or Apple

The diagnostic data tell the developer how your smartphone is performing to help them produce better products. You have the option to enable this feature when setting up your device. Whenever you need to save battery life, follow the steps below to disable this option.

- Go to the Settings app.

- Click on **Privacy.**
- Then go to **Analytics** and shift the sliders to the left to disable this feature.

Disable Vibrations

When you place your device on vibration, the phone vibrates at every notification that comes into the device. The whole process involved in this causes the battery life to go low. Follow the steps below to turn off vibrations:

- Go to the Settings app.
- Click on **Sounds & Haptics**
- Then move the slider beside **Vibrate on Ring** to the left to disable.

Other Helpful Tips to Improve the Longevity of Your iPhone Battery

Several factors can reduce the life of your battery, like leaving your phone plugged in even after the battery is fully charged. I have compiled the list below to help you prolong your battery life.

- Do not wait for your battery to drain before charging it. Do not let the phone battery drop to below 20% before you charge.
- Do not expose the smartphone to excess heat. Avoid charging your device in a scorching environment.
- If for any reason, you do not intend to use your phone for about a week and above, ensure that the battery goes below 80% but not below 30 percent. Then shut down the phone properly before setting aside.

- Moving your phone quickly from a very hot to a very cold condition can affect the health of the battery.
- You do not need to always fully charge your phone, as it can aid in damaging your battery.

Chapter 26: Troubleshooting the iPhone 11 Device

In this section, we will look at every possible challenge you may have with the iPhone and the solutions.

Most minor issues that occur with the iPhone can be resolved by restarting the device or doing a soft reset. If the soft reset fails to solve the problem, then you can carry out other resets like the hard reset and master reset. Here, you will learn how to use each of the available reset methods.

Restart/ Soft Reset iPhone

This is by far the most prevalent solution to most problems you may encounter on the iPhone. It helps to remove minor glitches that affect apps or iOS as well as gives your device a new start. This option doesn't delete any data from your phone; you will have your contents intact once the phone comes up.

Method 1:

- Hold both the side and Volume Down (or Volume Up) keys at the same time until the slider comes up on the screen.
- Move the slider to the right for the phone to shut down.
- Press the **Side** button until the Apple logo shows on the screen.
- Your iPhone will reboot.

Method 2:

- Go to **Settings** then **General.** Click on **Shut Down.**
- This will automatically shut down the device.

- Wait for some seconds, then Hold the **Side** button to start the phone.

Hard Reset/ Force Restart an iPhone

There are some cases when you need to force restart your phone. These are mostly when the screen is frozen and can't be turned off, or the screen is unresponsive. Just like the soft reset, this will not wipe the data on your device. It is important to confirm that the battery isn't the cause of the issue before you begin to fore-restart.

Follow the steps below to force-restart:

- Press the **Volume Up** and quickly release.
- Press the **Volume Down** and quickly release.
- Hold down the Side button until the screen goes blank and then release the button and allow the phone to come on.

Factory Reset your iPhone (Master Reset)

A factory reset will erase every data stored on your iPhone and return the device to its original form from the stores. Every single data from settings to personal data saved on the phone will be deleted. You should create a backup before you go through this process. You can either backup to iCloud or iTunes. Once you have successfully backed up your data, please follow the steps below to wipe your phone.

A factory reset will erase every data stored on your iPhone and return the device to its original form. Every single data from settings to personal data saved on the phone will be deleted. You should create a backup before you go through this process. Once you have successfully backed up your data, please follow the steps below to wipe your phone:

- From the **Home** screen, click on **Settings.**
- Click on **General**.
- Select **Reset**.
- Chose the option to **Erase All Content and Settings**.
- When asked, enter your passcode to proceed.
- Click **Erase iPhone** to approve the action.

Depending on the volume of data on your phone, it may take some time for the reset to finish.

Once the reset is done, you may choose to set up with the **iOS Setup Assistant/Wizard** where you can choose to restore data from a previous iOS or proceed to set the device as a fresh one.

Use iTunes to Restore the iPhone to factory defaults

Another alternative to reset your phone is by using iTunes. To do this, you need a computer, either Mac or Windows, that has the most current version of the iOS as well as has installed the iTunes software. A factory reset is advisable as a better solution to major issues that come up from software that wasn't solved by the soft or force restart. Although you will lose data, however, you get more problems fixed, including software glitches and bugs. Follow the guide below once all is set:

- Use the lightning cable or USB to connect your device to the computer.

- Open the iTunes app on the computer and allow it to recognize your device.
- Look for and click on your device from the available devices shown on iTunes.
- If needed, chose to back up your phone data to iTunes or iCloud on the computer.
- Once done, tap the **Restore** button to reset your iPhone.
- A prompt will pop-up on the screen, click **Restore** to approve your action.
- Allow iTunes to download and install the new software for your device.

I Can't Activate my Mobile Phone

There are four possible reasons for this. Causes and solutions are listed below:

- If the activation was not done correctly, repeat the activation steps as instructed in this book

- There may be a temporary problem with your network connection. Wait for some time and try again or you can move to any location and then try again.

- The problem may be with the SIM card. If so, contact your carrier's customer service for assistance.

Chapter 27: Conclusion

With all the teachings in this book, I am confident that you will be able to enjoy to the fullest all the fantastic features of the iPhone 11. The iPhone 11 is not only a phone for making and receiving calls. With the right knowledge on use the iPhone 11, you can turn it to your office and achieve greater things with this device.

If you are pleased with the content of this book, don't forget to recommend this book to a friend.

Thank you.

Printed in Great Britain
by Amazon

49121516R00097